Northern Ireland

Republic of Ireland

DONEGAL

DERRY

ANTRIM

TYRONE

FERMANAGH

DOWN

ARMAGH

SLIGO

MONAGHAN

MAYO

LEITRIM

CAVAN

LOUTH

ROSCOMMON

LONGFORD

MEATH

WESTMEATH

GALWAY

OFFALY

DUBLIN

KILDARE

LAOIS

WICKLOW

CLARE

CARLOW

TIPPERARY

KILKENNY

WEXFORD

LIMERICK

WATERFORD

KERRY

CORK

THE NEW IRISH TABLE
RECIPES FROM IRELAND'S TOP CHEFS

THE NEW IRISH TABLE

RECIPES FROM IRELAND'S TOP CHEFS

DARINA ALLEN ✦ MARTIN BEALIN
DERRY CLARKE ✦ ULTAN COOKE
KEVIN DUNDON ✦ CATHERINE FULVIO
NEVEN MAGUIRE ✦ NOEL McMEEL
IAN ORR ✦ TIM O'SULLIVAN

PHOTOGRAPHY BY CARSTEN KRIEGER ✦ CHRIS HILL ✦ AND OTHERS

Foreword by Tourism Ireland

Edited by Leslie Conron Carola

imagine!

An Imagine Book
Published by Charlesbridge
85 Main Street
Watertown, MA 02472
(617) 926-0329
www.charlesbridge.com

Project Director and Photo Researcher: Leslie Conron Carola, Arena Books Associates, LLC, www.arenabooksassociates.com
Design: Elizabeth Johnsboen, Lori S. Malkin
Cover Design and Layouts: Lori S. Malkin
Province Introductions: Peter Harbison

Library of Congress Cataloging-in-Publication Data
Names: Conron Carola, Leslie.
Title: The new Irish table : recipes from Ireland's top chefs / compiled by Leslie Conron Carola.
Description: Watertown, MA : Charlesbridge, 2017.
Identifiers: LCCN 2016032631 (print) | LCCN 2016033055 (ebook)
    | ISBN 9781623545246 (hardback) | ISBN 9781632892119 (ebook) | ISBN 9781632892126 (ebook pdf)
Subjects: LCSH: Cooking, Irish. | BISAC: COOKING / Regional & Ethnic /Irish. | COOKING / Courses & Dishes / General. | COOKING / Entertaining. |
LCGFT: Cookbooks.
Classification: LCC TX717.5 .N49 2017 (print) | LCC TX717.5 (ebook) | DDC 641.59417—dc23
LC record available at https://lccn.loc.gov/2016032631

Coole Swan is a registered trademark of Coole Quay Liqueur Company; Guinness is a registered trademark of Guinness & Company; Irish Mist liqueur is a registered trademark of C&C International, Ltd.; Kerrygold is a registered trademark of Irish Dairy Board Cooperative Limited; Shortcross Gin is a registered trademark of Rademon Estate Distillery.

The recipes have been contributed by the chefs for Tourism Ireland. Copyright for each recipe is held by the individual chefs: Derry Clarke, Catherine Fulvio, Kevin Dundon, Darina Allen, Martin Bealin, Ultan Cooke, Tim O'Sullivan, Noel McMeel, Ian Orr, Neven Maguire. Copyright information for the recipes is included in the list of recipes by chefs on pages 232-233, considered a continuation of this copyright page. Photo credits are on page 239.

Visit www.Ireland.com to plan an unforgettable culinary trip through the Emerald Isle.

Printed in China
10 9 8 7 6 5 4 3 2 1

Contents

Foreword

This book is both a tribute to and a celebration of the island of Ireland and the exceptional contemporary culinary landscape. Ireland today is a paradise for epicures.

Ireland is known throughout the world for its warm, friendly welcome, magnificent landscapes, vibrant towns and villages with music-filled pubs, and something delicious at every turn. Come and see for yourself, immerse yourself in its rich heritage and culture, and let your imagination take flight.

Ireland's UNESCO Heritage sites offer a look at a fascinating history and culture. The 5,000-year-old Newgrange passage-tomb in Ireland's Ancient East predates the Egyptian pyramids by as many as 500 years. Visit one of Belfast's oldest attractions—St. George's Market, which has hosted a weekly market since 1604, an authentic foodie haven with more than 248 stalls overflowing with gorgeous produce. See the Giant's Causeway, along the Causeway Coastal route in Co. Antrim. Though history tells us this distinctive and breathtaking geological formation of thousands of basalt columns was created by volcanic activity millions of years ago, legend tells us otherwise.

ABOVE: Sheep yogurt mousse with sliced strawberries from Ultan Cooke at Ballynahinch.

RIGHT: The Giant's Causeway along the northern coast in Co. Antrim is an extraordinary collection of basalt columns. Legend tells us that this was the work of the legendary giant, Finn McCool.

Walk in the footsteps of Oscar Wilde or James Joyce, visit Dublin's famous Abbey Theater founded by W. B. Yeats, or stop by Trinity College to view the Book of Kells. Drive along the Wild Atlantic Way, the world's longest defined coastal touring route, spanning from Co. Donegal down to Kinsale, Co. Cork. Visit the local markets along the route to meet the artisan producers. Experience the majestic coastal vistas from the Cliffs of Moher that rise 700 feet from the sea in Co. Clare. For the adventurous at heart take a boat ride to Skellig Michael's monastic ruins founded in the 6th century and located just off the coast of Kerry. George Bernard Shaw commented that it was an "incredible, impossible, mad place . . . part of our dream world."

All of these sites are inviting. But there is another lure. There has been a culinary renaissance in Ireland. Without doubt, Ireland today is a food-lover's choice. Artisan food-producers and chefs concentrate on fresh, local, seasonal produce offering an enticing contemporary taste.

The top chefs included in this book—Darina Allen, Martin Bealin, Derry Clarke, Ultan Cooke, Kevin Dundon, Catherine Fulvio, Neven Maguire, Noel McMeel, Ian Orr, and Tim O'Sullivan—are great ambassadors for Ireland. They take pride in sourcing the best local, seasonal produce and preparing it with creative inventiveness. Many of these chefs trained in Ireland, extended their training far from home, and brought that experience back to the island of Ireland.

Let this book whet your appetite to come and experience the island and its exciting food first hand.

—Ruth Moran, *Tourism Ireland*

ABOVE: The lush green valleys of the Burren push up against the limestone-covered hills, providing a stunning stage for a setting sun.

BELOW: Ian Orr from Browns in Derry putting the finishing touches on the seared scallops and potato bread for our photo shoot.

Introduction

Ireland—a small island steeped in beauty and history lies on the north-western edge of the Atlantic Ocean on the same latitude as Newfoundland. You would expect a cold, icy environment, but the Gulf Stream running the full length of the west coast of Ireland brings a temperate climate (with lots of rain and lots of sun) producing lush flower gardens, wild-flower-studded grass fields, amazing fresh vegetables and fruit, and animals grazing on the sweet grass for up to 300 days a year. Ireland offers an extraordinary bounty of natural foods, from vegetables and fruit to meats (lamb, beef, pork, and venison), fish, cheese, butter, and milk.

ABOVE: An early morning seacoast in Galway, Co. Connacht.

Ireland is a stunning landscape of contrasts, wild and gentle: a wind-rattled, cloud-kissed magical meeting of sea and land; the haunting, lyrical stillness of ancient monuments prominent on the landscape, or a solitary boat on a still lake; crumbling castles by mysterious lakes; lovely wild sea pinks growing on the cliffs by the sea; thunderous waves crashing over rocks. Travelers to Ireland have always extolled the stunning landscape with its powerful mythic presence, the vibrant towns and cities, and the warmth of the people, but they have rarely mentioned the food. Ireland has become more culturally diverse in recent years and the culinary landscape reflects this broadening trend.

We have gathered recipes from some of the finest chefs in Ireland in this celebration of Ireland and its food today. These chefs have transformed the culinary landscape of Ireland with an ethos of fresh, local, seasonal foods prepared simply. An abundance of fresh produce is not new to Ireland, but food lovers are responding to the exciting treatment of those fine ingredients. Every one of the outstanding chefs selected from all four provinces offers an imaginative style of food preparation, demonstrating respect for the old while adding their own contemporary creativity to the process. Each of these chefs connects with the environment; they are masters at using local ingredients from the miles of farmland and the surrounding sea, lakes, and plentiful rivers carving through the land. The new wave of artisan producers and imaginative chefs work together as a team. It's all a team—the earth and its splendid fare, the farmers and producers, the chefs with the seasonal, natural ethos. Today, Ireland is a real food destination,

and these chefs are ambassadors for Ireland.

Our chefs demonstrate that the culinary artisan food culture is country-wide, stretching from coast to coast, east to west, north to south. There is variety in the style of food presentation: some are as casual as an easy dinner at home, others are stylishly sculpted for a fine restaurant. From no-fuss style to elegantly staged productions—there is room for all.

Dishes prepared for a restaurant differ certainly from what we cook every day at home. Each of these chefs looks at the core of a dish and then adds embellishments. A lesson we can learn from this is to use our imagination rather than be tied to exactly how a dish is shown here. Be flexible, use your imagination—and your own local foods. The chefs offer what they do with *their* fresh, local, seasonal produce. You should do the same.

Some of the recipes included are signature dishes from the chefs and may have appeared in their own books or been included in a television cooking show or taught in their cooking schools. Only in this book, however, do we witness the breadth of the artisanal food movement in Ireland in the hands of chefs Darina Allen and Kevin Dundon and Martin Bealin and Catherine Fulvio and Derry Clarke and Ultan Cooke and Ian Orr and Noel McMeel and Neven Maguire and Tim O'Sullivan.

The cultivated range of artisan food producers and chefs has made the farm-to-fork concept an exciting reality. This book is a treasury of food in Ireland today.

NOTE: We have included metric measurements and oven temperature equivalents for those who use them. The conversions are approximate, and they have been rounded up.

ABOVE: The mesmerizing stillness of a quiet lake in Killarney, Co. Kerry at day's end is literally a pause for reflection.

BELOW: Derry Clarke at l'Ecrivain in Dublin preparing salmon with avocado cream and vegetables for our photoshoot.

Meet the Chefs

DARINA ALLEN An Irish chef, food writer, television personality, and founder of Ballymaloe Cookery School, Darina is the author of many cookbooks. Her *Ballymaloe Cooking School Cookbook* was nominated for Best International Cookbook by the James Beard Foundation. A member of the International Association of Cooking Professionals, Euro-Toques, the Irish Food Writer's Guild, the Consumer Foods and Ingredients Board of *An Bord Bia*, and on the Food Safety Board of Ireland, she has appeared on *Good Morning America* and other US television programs.

MARTIN BEALIN After qualifying as a chef in 1988, Martin Bealin honed his skills in kitchens worldwide before returning to Ireland to open the now famous Global Village Restaurant in Dingle, Co. Kerry in 1997. The restaurant, which he runs with his wife Nuala, has won numerous awards and is now in the top 5 Seafood Restaurants on the island. Bealin is passionate about using the finest produce on his doorstep. Fish and shellfish from the surrounding seas are a speciality, as is Kerry mountain lamb and beef. He grows his own fruits and vegetables for the restaurant. Martin was the 2012 winner of Best Restaurant and Best Chef in Munster.

DERRY CLARKE One of Ireland's leading Michelin-starred chefs, Derry Clarke was born in Dublin and trained in classical French tradition at Man Friday in Kinsale. Award-winning chef, cookbook author, TV and radio personality, active member and former Commissioner General of Euro-Toques, Ireland, Derry and his wife Sallyanne own and run L'Ecrivain restaurant in Dublin. Awards won for innovative culinary skills include Evian Food and Wine's Best Restaurant and Best Restaurant in Dublin for two succeeding years, the Bushmills Dining in Ireland Guide's Best Restaurant and Best Chef. Derry was elected into *Food & Wine* magazine's "Hall of Fame."

ULTAN COOKE Galway native Ultan Cooke is Head Chef at Ballynahinch Castle in Galway, along the Wild Atlantic Way, Ireland's spectacular coastal route from Donegal to West Cork. He studied and trained in the west of Ireland before heading to London where he worked at Smiths of Smithfield, ending up as Head Chef, and then to The Luxe. Ultan was formerly Head Chef at Michelin-starred Aniar restaurant in Galway. Aniar won its Michelin star before Ultan arrived but it was maintained under his creative direction.

KEVIN DUNDON Award-winning co-proprietor with his wife, Catherine, of Dunbrody House and Restaurant, Cookery School and Spa; chef and partner of the Disney World, Florida Raglan Road Irish Gastropub; cookbook author, and primetime cooking show regular, Kevin Dundon is an authority member of Fáilte Ireland, Ireland's national tourism board. After graduating from catering college, he worked in Switzerland, at the Fairmont Hotels in Canada, and then back to Ireland as the youngest Executive Chef at Dublin's Shelburne Hotel. Four years later he and his wife opened Dunbrody, named Restaurant of the Year three times.

CATHERINE FULVIO Award-winning TV chef, food writer, and proprietor of four-star Ballyknocken House and Cookery School, Catherine Fulvio grew up on the family's 280-acre working farm in Co. Wicklow developing an authentic connection with food and the land, seen in her well-honed "field-to-fork" food philosophy. Catherine uses only the best of local and seasonal produce at Ballyknocken, often their own herbs, vegetables, and fruit. A recognized TV presence, Catherine has appeared in many countries including the UK, France, U.S. (*The Today Show*), Australia, and New Zealand.

NEVEN MAGUIRE Neven Maguire trained in some of the highest-profile restaurants in the world: Roscoff in Belfast, The Grand Hotel in Berlin, Lea Linster in Luxembourg, and Arzac Restaurant in San Sebastian. In 2001 Neven took over the family business, and turned a local restaurant in the rural village of Blacklion in Co. Cavan into a national phenomenon. Along the way he has produced numerous cookbooks and has become a television celebrity chef. He hosts a cooking show on PBS *Create TV.* Neven is the winner of Best Chef and MacNean House has been named Ulster's Best Restaurant.

NOEL McMEEL Noel's celebrity credentials include cooking for the 2013 G8 conference at Lough Erne Resort in Northern Ireland and five celebration dinners at the James Beard Foundation. Training at the Northern Ireland Hotel and Catering College in Portrush, Noel worked with Paul and Jeanne Rankin at Roscoff in Belfast; a 1988 scholarship to the US led to stints at The Watergate Hotel in Washington, DC, with Jean Louis Palladin and Chez Panisse in Berkeley, working with his culinary heroine, chef-patron Alice Waters. Noel won *The Sunday Independent* Irish Restaurant Award's Best Chef in Ulster in 2011.

IAN ORR Derry-born Ian Orr, multi-award-winning Head Chef and co-owner of Browns in Derry trained under the late Robbie Millar at Northern Ireland's Michelin-starred Shanks before moving to London's River Cafe and then to Rathmullan House Hotel in Donegal as Head Chef. His passion for good local produce and seasonality, and his culinary skill have caught the attention of food writers and experts resulting in several awards and listings in leading food guides. He was the Winner of Ireland's Chef of the Year 2013 from Georgina Campbell, and Browns has been named Best Restaurant in Derry and in Ulster.

TIM O'SULLIVAN Head Chef for over twenty years at Renvyle House near the Wild Atlantic Way in Connemara, one of the top culinary spots in the country, Tim O'Sullivan has been a Commissioner of Euro-Toques, Ireland, a driving force in Ireland's food revolution, and a supporter of local produce. Tim's background of classic Irish and European cooking has blended well with newer trends to produce dishes that show contemporary Irish cuisine at its best. He has won Best Chef in Connacht in 2007 and 2008, from Georgina Campbell and from *Food & Wine* magazine.

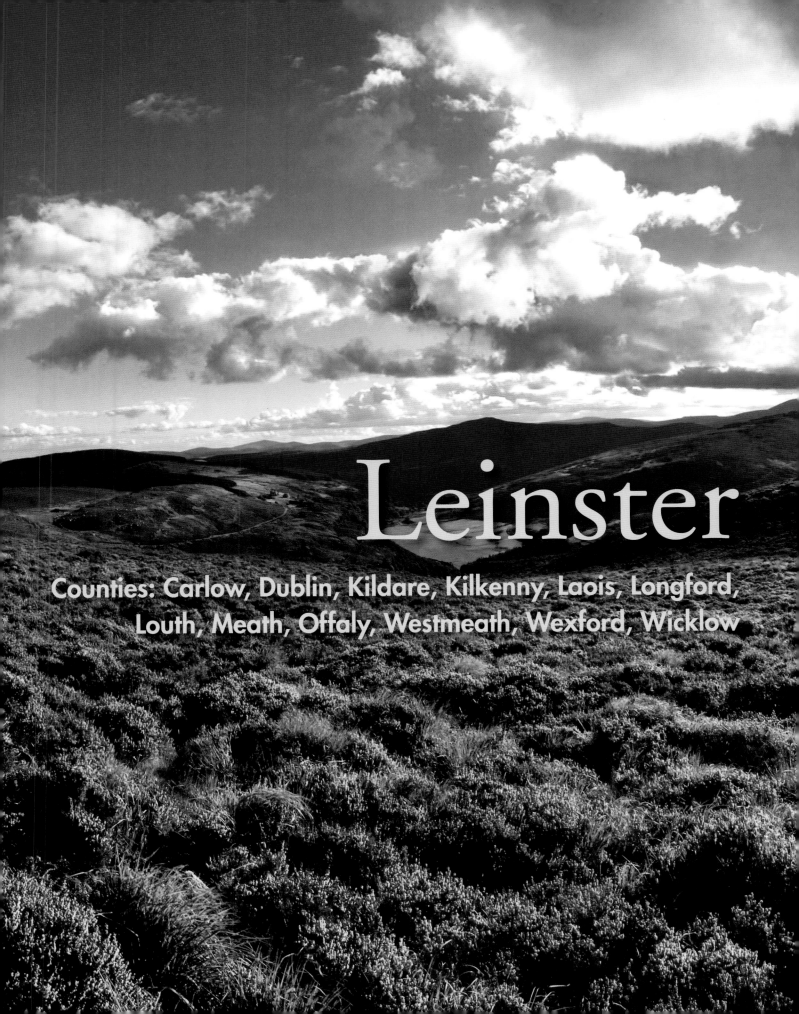

Leinster

Counties: Carlow, Dublin, Kildare, Kilkenny, Laois, Longford, Louth, Meath, Offaly, Westmeath, Wexford, Wicklow

PREVIOUS SPREAD: Hills of jewel-toned heather thrive under a summery sky in Co. Wicklow, known as the "Garden of Ireland."

BELOW: Glendalough, the "Valley of Two Lakes," tucked into the rugged Wicklow Mountains is the serene hermitage founded by St. Kevin in the sixth century. The round tower reaching one hundred feet above the ground has been a beacon for travelers for centuries.

The province of Leinster, with a comparatively sunny climate and a population of over two million, occupies the midlands and south-eastern part of Ireland, and contains more counties than any other—Carlow, Dublin, Kildare, Kilkenny, Laois, Longford, Louth (the smallest of them), Meath, Offaly, Westmeath, Wexford and Wicklow. It is largely bounded by hills from Carlingford in the north to the Blackstairs in the south, with considerable mountain ranges between them in Dublin and Wicklow. More than any of the other provinces, Leinster has large flat areas beside the sea which facilitated access to the country for some of its earliest inhabitants ten thousand years ago. That low-lying terrain continues throughout the western part of the province as far as the river Shannon which divides it from Connacht, interrupted by the Slieve Bloom hills which provide a contrast in relief. The two major rivers entirely within the province, once rich in salmon, fall gently to the sea—the Boyne of historical significance and the Liffey which flows through Dublin to the coast. The fertile land of Leinster

ABOVE: The Boyne river moves slowly through the rich farm land of Co. Meath, site of the 5,000 year old Newgrange passage tomb. The ruins of the 15th century Dunmoe Castle are on the right.

LEFT: Fishing boats moored in the protection of a Wicklow town.

ABOVE: The newest bridge to span the river Liffey in Dublin is the extraordinary Samuel Beckett Bridge. Designed by Spanish architect Santiago Calatrava, it reportedly references the Irish harp, the official symbol of Ireland.

allows for plenty of tillage, encouraging the growth of wheat and barley which help the brewing and distilling industries. These are no longer concentrated solely in Dublin, however, with craft breweries now springing up all over the country. Dublin and Wicklow in particular could lay claim to the title of "The Garden of Ireland," as they are among the largest providers of vegetables and, to a lesser extent, fruit.

Being bordered on the east by the Irish Sea, the province was easy prey to invaders down the centuries, from the Nordic Vikings to their collateral descendants, the Normans, who made Dublin the center of English power in Ireland for seven hundred years, and which is now the capital of the Republic of Ireland. During the last few decades, Leinster in general and Dublin in particular have welcomed immigrants speaking many languages and bringing about changes, including a much greater variety of international cuisine.
—**Peter Harbison**

TOP: Sheep grazing in a lush green field overlooking the sea in Wexford.

RIGHT: Produce fresh from local farms are sold in an open-air street market in Dublin.

L'Ecrivain
Co. Dublin
Chef: Derry Clarke

BELOW: The entrance to l'Ecrivain on Lower Baggot Street in the center of Dublin.

BELOW RIGHT: Chef Derry Clarke.

Derry Clarke and his wife Sallyanne opened l'Ecrivain Restaurant in 1989. Derry and l'Ecrivain have received many awards over the years, such as Best Restaurant and Best Chef. L'Ecrivain is the proud holder of a Michelin Star, which was first awarded in 2003.

Derry Clarke reached international acclaim being inducted into *Food & Wine* magazine's "Hall of Fame" and granted a five-star review by *The New York Times* describing l'Ecrivain as "superb."

Derry promotes the use of organic food and non-genetically modified foods (non GMO). His food ethos is simple. He uses the finest of local, fresh produce, supporting small farmers and artisan producers.

MENUS

LUNCH

Crispy Duck Breast with Glazed Butternut Squash and Star Anise Jus

Lemon Curd with Meringue and Raspberries

DINNER ONE

Vodka-Cured Irish Salmon with Avocado Cream, Pickled Vegetables, and Horseradish Mayonnaise

Beef Fillet and Brisket with Morels and Mushroom Purée

Pear Mille Feuille

DINNER TWO

Cod, Octopus, Purple Broccoli, Broccoli Purée, and Horseradish Mayonnaise

Venison with Puréed Celeriac and Spinach

Chocolate Mousse with Walnut Ganache

Crispy Duck Breast with Glazed Butternut Squash and Star Anise Jus

OPTION: Purée some of the cooked butternut squash and add to the plate, along with the cubed, roasted butternut squash. For the photograph we added a blanched shallot or sweet onion in addition to the puréed squash, and a piece of the bacon sautéed. Dried spice or breadcrumbs complete the dish.

FOR THE GLAZED BUTTERNUT SQUASH
1 butternut squash, peeled and cubed
4 large shallots (peeled and halved)
Approximately 8 slices/200 g cured bacon, cut, blanched, and cubed
Juice of 1 orange
Juice of 1 lime
1 tbsp olive oil
4 tbsp butter
4 tbsp chopped fresh sage
4 tbsp chopped fresh thyme

FOR THE DUCK
4 duck breasts
1 tbsp honey
Sea salt and pepper

FOR THE STAR ANISE JUS
½ cup/100 g brown sugar
3½ fl oz/100 ml red-wine vinegar
2 oranges (juice and zest)
4 star anise, lightly crushed
8 fl oz/250 ml demi-glace or beef stock

Preheat oven to 350°F/180°C/Gas Mark 4.

Put butternut squash, shallots, and bacon in a bowl. Add orange juice, lime juice, olive oil, butter, sage, and thyme; season with sea salt and cracked black pepper. Toss all ingredients together and spread onto a roasting pan and bake in the preheated oven until tender, 15 to 20 minutes.

Put the duck breast skin side down on a cold heavy frying pan. Place on high heat and cook until the skin is crisp, about 5 minutes. Turn the duck breast over and put it in the oven. Reduce the heat to medium, and cook for 3 to 5 minutes further. This will cook the duck rare (pink). Cook longer for medium and well done. Remove from the oven and let cool. Brush the duck with the honey as it is resting.

To make the star anise jus, heat the sugar and vinegar in a sauce pan over a medium heat until it forms a brown caramel (do not overcook or the sauce will be bitter). Add the orange juice, star anise, and demi-glace or beef stock.

Simmer for 5 minutes over low heat. Strain, check the seasoning, and add the zest.

Allow the duck breast to rest for about 15 minutes, then carve lengthways. Spoon the vegetables onto four serving plates. Place duck on top and serve sauce on the side.

Serves 4

Lemon Curd with Meringue and Raspberries

FOR THE LEMON CURD
3 eggs
¾ cup/150 g sugar
Juice of 3 lemons (keep the rind)
8 tbsp butter
1 tbsp zest from the lemon rind

FOR THE MERINGUE
4 egg whites at room temperature
1 cup/220 g superfine sugar
Raspberries for garnish

Preheat oven to 325°F/170°C/Gas Mark 3.

Whisk eggs, sugar, and lemon juice in a bain marie until mixture becomes thick (200°F/71°C). Remove from the heat and push through a fine sieve into a bowl. Whisk in the butter bit by bit and add the zest. Cover with plastic wrap and cool in the refrigerator.

Place egg whites into a clean, dry mixing bowl. Whisk until you have soft peaks. Add sugar slowly and whisk to stiff peaks. Place in a piping bag. Pipe the meringues onto a baking tray and bake in the preheated low oven for 35 minutes. Brown the meringues if you wish by putting them under the broiler for a few seconds until they are a light golden color. Watch carefully. Remove from the oven and let the meringues cool for 1 to 2 minutes. Or brown the meringues, if you wish, with a culinary torch.

Remove the lemon curd from the refrigerator. Cut into individual servings or spoon into individual ramekins or glasses. Decorate with the piped swirls of meringue.

Garnish with fresh raspberries.

Serves 4

NOTE: A bain marie is a double boiler in which the top container holding food to be cooked gently is placed in a bath of simmering water. It can be a set of pots with one fitting snugly on top of the other, or the bottom container can be a larger pan holding a pool of warm water that comes about half way up the sides of the heat-proof cooking container(s). The wider, flat pan is useful when cooking severeal ramekins of food such as custard.

NOTE: This photograph shows a more formal, "dressed" or "staged" presentation of the lemon curd that we might present at the restaurant. The embellishments include raspberry purée, crushed pistachios, and some flowers, which would be a lovely touch for a grand dinner party at home. The basic lemon curd with meringue decoration is the heart of this recipe, a simple and elegant one for home cooks. At home, I usually keep the presentation simple, without all the garnish here.

Vodka-Cured Irish Salmon with Avocado Cream, Pickled Vegetables, and Horseradish Mayonnaise

NOTE: A loaf of brown bread and an iced shot of Grey Goose® are perfect accompaniments to this recipe.

SALMON

2¼ lb/1 kg salmon fillet
4 tbsp sea salt
4 tbsp sugar
1 orange, juice and rind
3 fl oz vodka
4 tbsp fresh dill
1 tbsp white peppercorns

Place salmon in a deep dish. Mix the salt and sugar together and sprinkle over the salmon, with the orange rind. Add the vodka and orange juice. Remove the dill leaves from the stalks and add the stalks

to the salmon. Chop the dill and set aside. Cover the salmon with plastic wrap and refrigerate overnight. Before serving rinse off the marinade in cold water and cover the salmon with the chopped dill. Slice the salmon and serve with brown bread and the iced Grey Goose.

AVOCADO CREAM
1 ripe avocado, skinned, halved, pit retained
2 tbsp crème fraîche
Juice of half a lemon
Salt and freshly ground white pepper

Blend the avocado, crème fraîche, and lemon juice together in a food processor. Season with salt and pepper to taste, then transfer to a bowl and place the avocado pit into the middle (this stops the avocado from turning brown). Cover the bowl tightly with plastic wrap and refrigerate.

PICKLED VEGETABLES
½ cup/100 g brown sugar
½ cup/120 ml white wine
1 cup good quality white-wine vinegar
1 tbsp whole star anise
4 bay leaves
1 tbsp fennel seeds
8 peeled baby carrots
8 pearl or baby onions
4 baby fennel or 1 large fennel cut into 4 pieces
½ cucumber, seeded and diced

In a pot, add sugar, wine, vinegar, star anise, bay leaves, and fennel seeds. Bring to a simmer and season (if it is too tart, add more sugar or if too sweet, add more vinegar). Add carrots, onions, and fennel, and simmer for 5 minutes. Add cucumber and season with salt and pepper to taste. Remove from heat. Allow the vegetables to cool in the liquid before removing.

HORSERADISH MAYONNAISE
Mix 4 tablespoons of mayonnaise with 1 tablespoon of horseradish (freshly grated or jar).

Slice the salmon and serve with a dollop of Avocado Cream and Pickled Vegetables on the side. Garnish with the horseradish mayonaise.

Serves 4

Derry Clarke garnishing the salmon plate with avocado cream.

Beef Fillet and Brisket with Morels and Mushroom Purée

Derry Clarke with Tom Doyle

Derry Clarke (right) with l'Ecrivain Head Chef Tom Doyle (left).

NOTE: For a very special occasion, heat a knob of butter in a pan, add truffles, and toss for 1 minute. Season and serve.

NOTE: The basic recipe is the meat and mushroom purée. Experiment with garnishes as you like.

FOR THE BRISKET
2–3 tbsp vegetable oil
2¼ lb/1kg beef brisket
1 onion, diced
1 stick celery
1 carrot, peeled and diced
2 cloves garlic, crushed
1 small leek, diced
5 fl oz/150 ml red wine
3½ fl oz/100 ml balsamic or
    red-wine vinegar
15 fl oz/450 ml beef or chicken stock
Salt and pepper to taste

FOR THE FILLET
12 oz/250 g beef fillet
2 tbsp vegetable oil

FOR THE MORELS AND MUSHROOMS
8 morels
Scant ½ lb/200 g button
    mushrooms
3½ fl oz/100 ml cream
½ tsp truffle oil

Heat 2 tbsp oil over medium-high heat in a pan large enough to hold the brisket. Add the brisket and sear on both sides. Season with salt and pepper and add the onion, celery, carrot, garlic, and leek. Cook for 2 to 3 minutes. Add the wine, vinegar, and stock. Cover with a lid and cook over a low heat for 3 hours until tender.

Heat 2 tbsp oil in a pan over high heat. Season the fillet with salt and pepper on both sides and brown on each side for 3 minutes. Remove from the heat and leave to rest.

Fry the morels and mushrooms in ½ tbsp oil in a pan until golden brown. Remove the morels and set aside. Strain out the liquid and put the mushrooms back in the pot. Add the cream and reduce over low heat until it has almost evaporated. Purée in a food processor, season with salt and pepper, and add ½ teaspoon truffle oil.

Serve the beef brisket and fillet with mushroom purée. Garnish with the morels.

Serves 4

NOTE: Mushroom purée sits in the roasted onion leaf in the center of the photograph. The brown dollop at the lower left is carmelized onion purée.

Pear Mille Feuille

NOTE: Save the liquid to use in a cocktail.

PEAR PURÉE
½ cup/100 g sugar
Juice of 1 orange
Juice of 1 lemon
4 pears, peeled and chopped into small squares
1 vanilla pod

Place sugar in a pot and heat gently until it turns a golden caramel color. Add the juice of 1 orange and 1 lemon, stir and add the chopped pears and vanilla pod. Leave to cool and drain excess liquid.

PASTRY
1 package of puff pastry
1 cup/100 g confectioners' sugar to dust and roll
1¼ cups/200 g hazelnuts, chopped

Preheat oven to 350°F/180°C/Gas Mark 4.

Roll out one sheet of puff pastry with confectioners' sugar until quite thin, then cut to 3 x 1½ in/8 x 4 cm pieces. Cook between two flat trays with parchment on either side for 9 minutes.

For the top layer, place a whole sheet (the size of a baking pan) of puff pastry on a baking pan and cover with a wire rack so it does not puff up too much. Cook for about 18 minutes or until golden. When cool, cut to 2 x 1¼ in/7 x 3 cm (the individual ones would have shrunk to this size). Dust with confectioners' sugar.

CUSTARD
8 fl oz/250 ml pear purée
⅓ cup/75 g sugar
5 large egg yolks, 3 oz/80 g egg yolk,
2 tbsp cornstarch
2 leaves gelatin or 1¼ tsp gelatin powder
3½ fl oz/100 ml whipped cream

In a medium bowl, mix the egg yolk and sugar, then whisk in the cornstarch until smooth.

Soak gelatin leaves in a bowl of cold water until soft. Or, if using powdered gelatin, sprinkle the powder on ¼ cup of cold water and set aside to set.

Bring the pear purée to a boil. Pour half into the egg mixture while whisking, then pour the pear and egg mixture back into the pot, whisking until it boils. Remove from the heat. Squeeze excess water from the gelatin leaves and add the leaves to the pear mixture (or add the set powdered gelatin), stirring well until the mixture is smooth. Place the mixture in a bowl, cover, and chill in the refrigerator for about an hour. Remove from the refrigerator, whisk gently to loosen, and fold in lightly whipped cream. Place in a piping bag.

To serve, place the cooked puff pastry on the plate and pipe the custard on top of the pastry. Add the second layer in the same way. Dust the top of the pastry with confectioners' sugar. Dress the plate with dollops of custard and chopped hazelnuts.

Serves 4

Cod, Octopus, Purple Broccoli, Broccoli Purée, and Horseradish Mayonnaise

NOTE: Court bouillon is an aromatic broth made with herbs and root vegetables used for poaching fish and other simple foods.

NOTE: Mussels, clams, or any other shellfish would be excellent alternates for the octopus.

NOTE: For cooking at home, I would keep the dish simpler—just the basic sautéed cod and broccoli—without the octopus or even the broccoli purée. The photo, opposite, is embellished for restaurant diners.

FOR THE OCTOPUS
2 qts/2 L court bouillon
1 octopus (2 lb/1 kg)

4 tbsp butter
1 tsp chopped parsley (or dill)
Salt and pepper

FOR THE HORSERADISH
MAYONNAISE
1 egg yolk
1 tsp mustard
1 lemon
⅔ cup/150 ml vegetable oil
     plus more to sauté the cod
3 tbsp/40 g horseradish, grated

FOR THE BROCCOLI PURÉE
2 medium size heads of
     broccoli, shaved and
     cleaned

FOR THE COD
4 cod fillets

FOR THE PURPLE BROCCOLI
¼ lb/100 g purple sprouting
     broccoli

In a deep pot, add the court bouillon and the octopus and simmer for 1½ hours until tender. Remove and chill. Portion octopus into 1½ in/4 cm pieces.

Place the egg yolk into a small bowl and add the mustard and a squeeze of lemon juice. Slowly whisk in the vegetable oil until thick. Season with salt and pepper to taste, and add the grated horseradish.

Bring a pot of water to boil and add a little salt. Cut and blanch the 2 heads of broccoli in the salted water for 2 minutes. Remove and squeeze out the excess water with a kitchen cloth or towel. Discard the water. Place the broccoli in a food processor and blend until smooth. Season and chill to keep a bright green color.

Season the fish fillets with salt and pepper.

Heat a pan with a little oil on a high heat, and place the cod skin side down and turn heat to low. Cook for about 4 minutes until the skin is crisp and golden. Turn the fish over, add butter and lemon juice, and cook for 1 minute.

NOTE: Purple broccoli loses most of its purple color when cooked.

Bring a pot of water to boil and cook the purple broccoli for 1½ minutes until tender. Season.

Heat broccoli purée in a pot until warm.

Heat a little butter in a pan and toss the octopus pieces in the butter until warm. Season with salt and pepper, and add a teaspoon of chopped parsley or dill.

To serve, place a few spoons of broccoli purée and some purple broccoli on a plate and arrange a cod fillet on top. Garnish with the octopus and horseradish mayonaise.

Serves 4

NOTE:
Homemade demi-glace takes a long time to prepare. Store-bought versions are available.

Venison with Puréed Celeriac and Spinach

1 head of celeriac
3½ fl oz/100 ml milk
8 tbsp butter
Salt and white pepper
½ lemon, juiced
Generous lb/500 g baby spinach
3½ fl oz/100 ml cream
Grated nutmeg
3½ fl oz/100 ml demi-glace
1 loin of venison
Bunch of watercress

Peel celeriac, dice into 1¼ in/3 cm cubes, and cook in a pan with the milk and butter on a low heat until cooked and tender. Once cooked, strain out the remaining milk/butter mix, crush the celeriac with a potato masher and add a little of the milk/butter mix back in until the celeriac is creamy but not too wet. Season with salt, white pepper, and a squeeze of lemon juice.

Bring a pot of salted water to a boil. Add the baby spinach for 10 seconds, then remove the spinach and squeeze out the excess water with a towel. Place in a blender with the cream and grate some fresh nutmeg into it. Once smooth, season the purée with salt and pepper and pass through a sieve. Cool to keep the green color.

For the loin of venison, trim off any excess fat. Season with salt and pepper. Sear on a hot pan with oil and butter making sure to turn the loin over every 10 to 20 seconds for about 2 to 3 minutes. Leave the loin to rest for 10 minutes in a warm place and slice into 4 portions.

Warm the spinach purée and crushed celeriac in two separate pots.

To serve, form a quenelle (a smooth egg-shaped dollop) or place a simple dollop of the celeriac on a plate. Add the sliced venison and a swirl of spinach purée and demi-glace. Garnish with a sautéed nectarine (or any fruit), watercress, and a few spoonfuls of demi-glace.

Serves 4

Tom Doyle constructing the finished plate.

Chocolate Mousse with Walnut Ganache

NOTE: A stock syrup is made by mixing sugar and cold water (2 cups of sugar to 2½ cups of water) in a pan and warming over a gentle heat. Then bring to a boil for 2 minutes. Remove from the heat and let it cool. Store in the refrigerator until ready to use.

NOTE: This is a sophisticated, dressed-up presentation. I like to serve the basic mousse with a scoop of raspberry sorbet for a lovely, simple presentation at home.

MOUSSE
3 egg yolks
3½ fl oz/100 ml stock syrup
1 cup/225 g melted milk chocolate
2 cups/450 ml lightly whipped cream

Whisk the egg yolks and stock syrup over a bain maire for 5 minutes (350°F/180°C) then continue to whisk in a blender until cool. Slowly add the melted chocolate and then fold in the whipped cream. Place in the refrigerator to set.

WALNUT GANACHE
¼ cup/50 g walnuts
5 oz/133 g white chocolate
10 fl oz/300 ml cream

Toast the walnuts and blend until you get a runny paste. Place the walnut paste and white chocolate in a bowl. Bring cream to boil and pour over the chocolate and walnut paste. Let this cool and then whisk to a whipped cream consistency.

CHOCOLATE CRUMB
4–5 chocolate cookies, crumbled with a rolling pin to desired consistency

TOASTED WALNUTS
1½ cups/300 g walnuts

Toast the walnuts on a cookie sheet in a 350°F/180°C/Gas Mark 4 oven for 8 to 10 minutes. Crush half and leave half whole as garnish.

Transfer the cooled mousse to a platter, and cover with chocolate crumb. Pipe several walnut and white chocolate ganache meringue-like dollops around the mousse. Garnish with the toasted walnuts, and more chocolate if you like.

Serves 4

Ballyknocken House and Cookery School
Glenealy, Ashford
Co. Wicklow
Chef: Catherine Fulvio

RIGHT: The entrance to Catherine Fulvio's Ballyknocken Cookery School in Co. Wicklow.

MENUS

LUNCH

Orange, Spinach, and Salmon Salad

TEA

Ballyknocken Tea Scones

Guinness® Chocolate Cupcakes

DINNER ONE

Carrot, Potato, and Cumin Soup

**Beef and Wicklow Wolf Stout Casserole
with Dumplings**

Apple and Mango Crumble

DINNER TWO

Seared Lamb and Beetroot Salad

Salmon and Leek Pie

Irish Mint Truffle Torte with Irish Mist Cream

BELOW: Catherine Fulvio with fresh vegetables just picked from the garden at Ballyknocken.

Catherine Fulvio is a celebrity chef, award-winning food writer, and proprietor of Ballyknocken House and Cookery School in Co. Wicklow.

The lush herb, vegetable, and soft fruit gardens of this 280-acre farm provide the food served in Ballyknocken House and the ingredients used in the state-of-the-art, award-winning Ballyknocken Cookery School. Catherine's deep connection with the land, encouraged by growing up here on a working farm, means her philosophy is focused on the importance of using the finest fresh, local, seasonal ingredients.

Catherine believes that cooking should be fun, and her hands-on, no-fuss, easy style make it so with warmth and enthusiasm. She appears on television often in Ireland, the UK, and in the US. Her television series has aired in over eleven countries.

Orange, Spinach, and Salmon Salad

Simple, healthy, and colorful, this is a delicious salad. It's perfect for a starter for dinner or as a main course for lunch. And it's all Irish—smoked salmon, delicious garden greens, and of course, potatoes!

FOR THE DRESSING
6 tbsp Irish rapeseed oil (or extra-virgin olive oil)
1 tbsp white-wine vinegar
1 tsp whole-grain mustard
1 orange, juice and zest
1 tsp sugar
Salt and freshly ground black pepper

FOR THE SALAD
4 oz/100 g each spinach and watercress
1 cucumber, sliced into ribbons
3 oranges, peeled and sliced
10 small potatoes, skin on, cooked and sliced in quarters
3 tbsp chopped chives
2 salmon fillets, poached and flaked
2 tsp finely chopped chives
A few dill sprigs to garnish.

NOTE: I love to add smoked trout instead of the salmon for another really delicious luncheon platter.

To make the dressing, place all the ingredients in a jar with a lid. Secure the lid tightly and shake well. Check the seasoning, and add a little more salt, sugar, or freshly ground black pepper if needed. Set aside.

Toss the spinach, watercress, and orange segments together, place on a large platter and drizzle with a little dressing. Arrange the potatoes on the salad leaves. Place the flaked poached salmon on top. Arrange the cucumber ribbons in between.

When ready to serve, pour some dressing over the salad. Sprinkle with chopped chives and a few fresh dill sprigs. Serve immediately.

Serves 4

Ballyknocken Tea Scones

There is nothing more mouthwatering than scones straight from the oven, butter melting onto them. Here we serve them with our signature rhubarb and ginger jam and on a "treat day," I'm even known to top with freshly whipped cream!

4½ cups/450 g cake flour
2 very heaping tsp baking powder
2 tbsp granulated sugar
8 tbsp chilled Kerrygold® salted butter
Approximately 10 fl oz/280 ml whole milk
Beaten egg and sugar to glaze

Preheat the oven to 450°F/230°C/Gas Mark 8.

Sift all the dry ingredients together. Rub in the chilled butter until the mixture resembles fine breadcrumbs. Make a well in the center and add most of the milk. Mix to a soft dough, adding all of the milk if required.

Place the dough onto a lightly floured surface and knead lightly. Roll out to about 1 inch/2½ cm thickness. Dip a scone cutter into flour and cut the dough into rounds of 1½ inch/4 cm.

Place the beaten egg in one bowl and the sugar in another. Dip the tops only of the scones into the egg first and then the sugar. Place on a floured baking pan, sugar side up. Then put the scones immediately into the hot oven for approximately 15 minutes, or until the scones rise and have a golden top. Enjoy them warm with Irish butter and homemade jam!

Makes about 17 scones, depending on the size.

NOTE: Prior to kneading, add cranberries or orange zest to the scone dough for a delicious treat.

Guinness® Chocolate Cupcakes

Strange as it may sound, Guinness and chocolate are a perfect combination. It's a rich smoothness that I hope you'll all love.

FOR THE CUPCAKES
6 fl oz/180 ml Guinness
¾ cup/180 g butter
⅓ cup/75 g cocoa powder, sifted
1 cup/225 g superfine sugar
2 eggs
1 tsp vanilla extract
¼ cup/60 ml milk
2¼ cups/285 g flour
2 tsp baking powder

FOR THE ICING
10 tbsp soft butter
1 tsp vanilla extract
Generous 2½ cups/350 g sifted confectioners' sugar
Chocolate shavings to decorate

Preheat the oven to 350°F/180°C/Gas Mark 4.

Arrange the cupcake liners in a muffin baking tray.

CUPCAKES
Pour the Guinness into a medium size saucepan, add the butter, and heat gently until melted. Remove from the heat. Stir in the cocoa powder and sugar.

In a bowl whisk together the eggs, vanilla extract, and milk.

Fold the flour and baking powder into the Guinness chocolate mix. Then add the egg, vanilla, and milk mixture to form a thick cake batter. Pour the batter into the cupcake liners in the cupcake pan, and put the tin into the preheated oven for 15 minutes until risen and cooked. Insert a skewer (or toothpick) into the middle of the cake and if it comes out clean, the cake is done. Leave to cool completely before decorating.

NOTE: To dress them up to serve with coffee, I make mini cupcakes and add an orange liqueur to the icing. They're delicious.

Whisk together the butter and vanilla extract using an electric beater, and slowly add the confectioners' sugar to form a fluffy icing. Spoon into a piping bag and pipe over the top of the cupcakes. Decorate with chocolate curls, if you wish.

Makes 12, depending on the size.

Carrot, Potato, and Cumin Soup

I chose this recipe because it reminds me so much of my childhood. When I was growing up here on the farm at Ballyknocken House, my mother made wonderful hearty soups, which we would devour after a morning's work feeding the animals! This was one of her favorite combinations. Our garden carrots here are so sweet they work well with the cumin.

NOTE: Fennel is also a wonderful combination with carrot. Simply replace the cumin with chopped fennel fronds and add 1 diced fennel bulb to the onions.

4 tbsp butter
4 cups/600 g carrots, chopped
2 small/200 g potatoes, peeled and chopped
1 cup/150 g onion, finely chopped
1 tsp ground cumin or to taste
Salt and freshly ground pepper
5 cups/1.1 L vegetable stock (may need more depending
    on weight of peeled vegetables)
4 tbsp cream

Melt the butter in a saucepan over low heat. Add the carrots, potatoes, and onions along with the cumin, salt, and pepper. Cover with a circle of parchment paper (or the wrapper from the butter) to retain the steam, and top with the saucepan lid. Leave to slowly simmer for about 10 minutes, stirring from time to time.

Add the stock. Increase the heat to bring it to a boil and then reduce to a simmer until the vegetables are soft.

Ladle into a blender, purée until smooth, and then return the purée to the saucepan to heat through. Check for seasoning, adding salt and pepper to taste, and add the cream.

Ladle into warm bowls and serve immediately with farmhouse soda bread.

Serves 6

Beef and Wicklow Wolf Stout Casserole with Dumplings

I cooked this dish on NBC's *Today Show* for St. Patrick's Day and it was a real success! Any good Irish stout works well in the recipes, but we are very fortunate in County Wicklow to have a number of artisan brewery developments. Combining our magnificent beef and the stout produces fabulous casseroles.

FOR THE STEW
3 lb/1.4 kg stewing beef, trimmed of fat, and cut unto 1½-inch cubes
Flour for dredging, with salt and pepper added
Irish rapeseed or extra-virgin olive oil
3 large onions, thinly sliced
2 tsp (1 dessertspoon) honey
1 tbsp Dijon mustard
1 medium can chopped tomatoes
1 tsp dried oregano
A bouquet garni (4 parsley sprigs, 2 fresh thyme sprigs, and
    1 bay leaf, tied together)
2 cups Wicklow Wolf Stout, or one you can obtain
Salt and freshly ground black pepper
Butter for sautéing mushrooms
2½ cups/275 g chestnut mushrooms, wiped and quartered

FOR THE DUMPLINGS
1 cup/100 g plain flour
1½ tsp baking powder
½ tsp salt
¼ tsp freshly ground black pepper
8 tbsp butter, diced
2 tbsp chopped chives and parsley
½ cup/120 ml milk
Egg wash, to glaze

NOTE: Wicklow Wolf Stout is from Wicklow Brewing Company, a local craft beproducer in Bray.

NOTE: Chestnut mushrooms are small white button mushrooms when immature, and lovely brown Portobello mushrooms when mature.

Preheat the oven to 350°F/180°C/Gas Mark 4.

To make the stew, roll the beef pieces in the flour. Heat some of the oil in a large frying pan and fry the beef in batches until browned on all sides. Place the browned meat into a deep, heavy-based saucepan. Add some more oil to the frying pan used to brown the beef and gently sauté the onions until softened. Deglaze the pan with some of the stout.

Add the sautéed onions, the stout and juices from the pan, the honey, mustard, chopped tomatoes, oregano, and bouquet garni to the saucepan. Bring to a boil, cover, reduce the heat to a simmer on a very low heat for about 2 hours or until the meat is tender. Stir gently from time to time. (It's also possible to cook in a casserole dish in the oven at a temperature of 350°F/180°C/Gas Mark 4.) In the meantime, quarter the mushrooms. Heat a large frying pan with butter, add the mushrooms, and season with salt and pepper; sauté until just cooked.

When the stew is cooked, add the mushrooms and simmer for 5 minutes. Check the seasoning, adding salt and freshly ground black pepper to taste.

Raise the oven to 450°F/230°C/ Gas Mark 8.

To make the dumplings, mix together the plain flour, baking powder, salt, and pepper in a bowl. Add the butter and rub it in with your fingers until it resembles fine breadcrumbs. Stir in the chives and parsley. Add enough milk to form a soft dough. Pat the dough out to 1 inch thick and, using a small scone cutter, shape into scones.

Carefully place the dumplings around the rim of the casserole and bake in the oven for about 15 minutes—depending on the dumpling size.

Garnish with chopped parsley when serving.

Serves 6

TIP: Without the dumplings, this casserole freezes very well, or you can prepare it 2 days ahead of time, chill, and allow the flavors to develop.

Apple and Mango Crumble

My grandparents planted the orchards here at Ballyknocken, so I've always been spoiled with all sorts of wonderful apple treats— from homemade apple jelly slathered on buttery toasted soda bread to my mother's famous apple pie! Here's one of my family favorites.

4 large Golden Delicious apples, peeled, cored, and diced
2 mangoes, peeled and diced
3 tbsp honey
1 small knob of crystallized ginger, very finely chopped
3 tbsp cold water

½ cup/65 g plain flour
½ cup/65 g whole-grain flour
6 tbsp chilled butter, diced
¼ cup/65 g soft brown sugar
6 walnuts, roughly chopped
3 tbsp sunflower seeds
⅓ cup/65 g oatmeal
Gently whipped fresh cream, to serve

Preheat the oven to 350°F/180°C/Gas Mark 4.

Brush an ovenproof gratin dish with melted butter, or you can brush ramekins or ovenproof jars if you want to make individual servings.

Place the apples, mangoes, honey, crystallized ginger, and water in a saucepan, cover and simmer on low heat for 5 minutes until the fruit is just softened.

To make the crumble topping, place the plain flour and whole-grain flour in a mixing bowl. Rub in the diced butter with your fingers until the mixture resembles breadcrumbs. Stir in the sugar, walnuts, sunflower seeds, and oatmeal.

Spoon the fruit into the ovenproof dish, jars, or ramekins. Add the crumble topping over the fruit. Bake in the preheated oven for about 20 to 25 minutes until golden brown (about 15 minutes for individual ramekins or jars). Serve warm with the lightly whipped cream.

Serves 4 to 6

NOTE: I sometimes opt for a ginger ice cream when I'm serving this crumble—it's a delicious pairing.

Seared Lamb and Beetroot Salad

County Wicklow is famous for lamb, and of course we are lamb farmers here at Ballyknocken. Not only that, but I'm always so delighted when our beets are in season in our garden. Lamb is at its best for flavor at the same time so it's a marriage made in heaven! I love the earthiness of the beets with the seared slices of juicy lamb and the sweetness from the honey coming through.

FOR THE DRESSING
8 tbsp Irish rapeseed (or extra-virgin olive) oil
4 tbsp white-wine vinegar
4 tsp whole-grain mustard or horseradish
2 tsp runny honey
Salt and pepper

FOR THE SALAD
9 oz/260 g lamb steak, seasoned with salt and
    freshly ground black pepper
Irish rapeseed (or extra-virgin olive) oil, for searing steak
2 small bunches watercress and/or fresh salad greens
3 medium cooked beets, sliced into wedges
Crusty breads, to serve

Preheat oven to 350°F/180°C/Gas Mark 4.

For the dressing, whisk together the oil, vinegar, mustard or horse-radish, and honey in a small bowl. Check for seasoning and add salt and pepper as desired.

Heat a skillet with a little oil and place the lamb steak in the pan; sear it on both sides. Leave to cook for about 2 minutes before removing from the pan. Cover and leave to rest for 5 minutes.

Arrange the watercress and/or salad greens on a serving platter; drizzle with some dressing. Place the beet wedges on top. Slice the lamb and arrange slices in between the beet wedges. Drizzle more dressing over the salad. Finish with cracked black pepper and fresh herbs. Serve with crusty bread.

Serves 4

NOTE: To cook the beets, place them washed and unpeeled, with a little salt, in a baking dish with cold water to cover the bottom of the pan about ¼ inch. Cover and bake the beets at 350°F/180°C/Gas Mark 4 for about 45 minutes to an hour, depending on the size of the beets. Remove from the oven and let them cool. Remove the skins—they will slip off easily at this point.

NOTE: I've also served slices of poached cinnamon pears in this salad in the autumn, and it's delicious.

Salmon and Leek Pie

This was my grandmother's favorite when we used to reserve Fridays for fish! It's a simple yet delicious dish. If you don't have any filo pastry, use a good quality ready-to-use puff pastry and cut fish shapes to place over the pastry top with egg wash and glaze.

Generous 1¼ lb/600 g salmon, diced into ¾ in/2 cm pieces
7 fl oz/225 ml milk
4 fl oz/125 ml cream
1 onion, finely sliced
1 fresh bay leaf
3 tbsp butter
2 leeks, thinly sliced
3 tbsp plain flour
1 tbsp chopped parsley
Salt and pepper to taste

6–7 sheets filo pastry
4 tbsp melted butter

Preheat the oven to 400°F/200°C/Gas Mark 6.

Lightly butter a medium-size gratin dish.

Place the salmon in a large pan and add the milk and cream. Add the onion and bay leaf and bring to a gentle boil. Reduce the heat and simmer for about 5 to 6 minutes or until the fish is cooked. Remove the fish from the pan and reserve the cooking liquid.

In the meanwhile, heat a large frying pan with a little butter, add the leeks and sauté for about 6 to 7 minutes, until softened but not brown.

To make the sauce, melt the butter in a saucepan. Stir in the flour and cook on low heat for 2 to 3 minutes. Slowly add the reserved cooking liquid (the milk and cream), stirring continuously. Season with salt and freshly ground black pepper. Stir in the chopped parsley.

Scatter the fish in the base of the buttered gratin dish, add the leeks, and cover with sauce. Place 1 sheet of the filo pastry over the salmon and leek mixture. Brush with melted butter. Scrunch the rest of the filo pastry and place on top of the sheet of pastry and brush with melted butter.

TIP: You can also use any firm white fish. Sometimes I'll add a few prawns and a splash of vodka for a great dinner party dish.

Bake for about 15 to 20 minutes until golden brown, but keep an eye on it as the pastry burns easily. Serve immediately with a garden salad.

Serves 4

Irish Mint Truffle Torte with Irish Mist Cream

This is my Irish-Italian combination, which has been a great hit in the cookery classes for years and years!

FOR THE TORTE
1 tbsp softened butter
5 tbsp ground almonds
   (1 for dusting the
   baking pan)
10 tbsp + 2 tsp butter
12 oz/350 g bittersweet
   chocolate (about 75%
   cocoa solid), chopped
6 sprigs fresh mint, washed
6 large eggs, at room
   temperature
6 tbsp granulated sugar

TO SERVE
2½ cups/500 ml cream,
   whipped
2 tbsp confectioners' sugar
3–4 tbsp Irish Mist® (or
   liqueur of your choice)
Cocoa to garnish

Preheat the oven to 350°F/180°C/Gas Mark 4.

Generously butter a 9-in/ 23-cm springform cake pan and lightly dust with about 1 tablespoon of the ground almonds. Wrap a double layer of aluminum foil around the exterior of the cake pan.

Melt the butter in a saucepan on a low heat and add the mint sprigs and leave to infuse for about 30 minutes. Then reheat and remove the mint leaves from the butter. Push the mint leaves through a sifter held over the saucepan to extract the mint oil to add back to the butter-mint mixture.

To melt chocolate, place about 2 in/5 cm of water in a saucepan and bring it to a simmer. Place a ceramic bowl on top of the saucepan (creating a bain marie). Note: the bottom of the bowl must not touch the water. Add the hot mint butter and the chocolate to the bowl over the simmering water. Stir from time to time until the chocolate is completely melted, then remove the bowl from the water. Set aside to cool slightly.

Meanwhile, beat the eggs and granulated sugar with an electric mixer on high speed for 8 to 10 minutes. It should quadruple in volume and become a light color, very thick and fluffy. This is very important; otherwise, the torte will be too flat.

Fold one-quarter of the egg mixture into the chocolate mixture; then very gently fold in the remaining egg and sugar mixture until it is incorporated. Carefully fold in the ground almonds.

Pour the batter into the prepared springform pan. Sit the springform pan into a baking or roasting pan to form a bain marie—a water bath in which to gently cook the cake. Put the baking pan with the cake in the springform pan on the center oven rack and pour enough water in the baking/roasting pan to come about 1½ in/½ cm up the sides of the cake pan. Bake for about 25 to 30 minutes. The top of the cake will lose its glossiness and be slightly mounded, but it should not bake so long that it rises and cracks. If you insert a skewer into the center it should come out slightly gooey.

Let the cake cool completely in the cake pan on a cooling rack. Before serving, run a knife around the edge of the cake and remove the outer ring.

Lightly whip the fresh cream, confectioners' sugar, and Irish Mist together. Dust the top of the cake with cocoa and serve with the flavored whipped cream. Fresh raspberries and a sprig of mint add a lovely touch.

Makes 1 cake, 12 servings

NOTE: Sometimes, I sprinkle raspberries over the torte before baking. They sink into the delicious chocolate gooiness; you'll need to add about 5 more minutes onto the baking time.

Dunbrody House
Arthurstown
Co. Wexford
Chef: Kevin Dundon

ABOVE: Dunbrody House front entrance bathed in a late afternoon winter sun.

Kevin Dundon, celebrated chef, cookbook writer, magazine contributor, and television guest is the joint proprietor with his wife, Catherine, of Dunbrody Country House Hotel and Restaurant on the Hook Peninsula on Ireland's southeast coast. Established in 1997 the multi award-winning Dunbrody Country House is considered one of Ireland's premier hotels and restaurants. His Dunbrody Cookery School is one of the most respected in the country.

MENUS

LUNCH

Potato, Prawn, and Lime Soup

Paupiette of Sole and Crabmeat

TEA

Victoria Sponge with Strawberries

DINNER ONE

Lobster Buttered Soup

Chicken Ballotines with Potato Farls

Wexford Berries with Mini Meringues

DINNER TWO

Scallops and Caviar with Nasturtium Coulis

Slow-Cooked Shoulder of Pork with Stuffing, Sautéed Potatoes, and Apple Compote

Buttermilk and Heather-Infused Panna Cotta

ABOVE: Kevin Dundon, Chef/Patron of Dunbrody House.

LEFT: In the kitchen garden at Dunbrody House.

Kevin's award-winning nine-part cooking show—*Modern Irish Food with Kevin Dundon*—aired on both RTE1 Ireland and PBS in the US. Kevin is also Chef/Patron of Raglan Road Irish Pub and Restaurant based in Orlando, Florida, a favorite of Disney World visitors.

The simple philosophy of both Dunbrody House and Dunbrody Cookery School is to produce fine food using only the best fresh, seasonal, locally-sourced ingredients.

Potato, Prawn, and Lime Soup

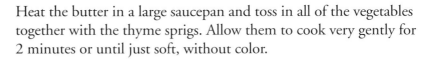

4 tbsp butter
5–6 large potatoes, chopped
1 carrot, peeled, left whole
1 medium onion
2 large sprigs of thyme
Salt and white pepper
4½ cups/1 L light prawn stock or vegetable stock
1 cup/240 ml pouring cream
1–2 limes, juice and zest
12 prawn tails, deveined and shelled

Heat the butter in a large saucepan and toss in all of the vegetables together with the thyme sprigs. Allow them to cook very gently for 2 minutes or until just soft, without color.

Next add in the stock and bring the mixture to a slow boil. Then reduce the heat and simmer for an additional 15 to 20 minutes or until the potatoes have softened completely. Remove the carrot, onion, and thyme from the mixture.

Using a hand blender, purée the soup until it is nice and smooth. Mix in the cream and return to the heat and bring back to a very gentle boil.

If you would like a thinner soup, now would be the best time to add any additional stock or cream to thin it down.

Add some lime juice and zest and correct the seasoning at this stage also.

Just before serving add the prawns to the soup and simmer for 2 minutes to just lightly cook the prawns.

Transfer the warm soup to your serving cups and garnish with a sprinkling of lime zest.

Serves 6

Paupiette of Sole and Crabmeat

6 skinless sole fillets, each approx. 3½ oz/100 g

FOR THE FILLING
4 tbsp butter
1 shallot, finely chopped
1 tbsp flour
3½ fl oz/100 ml white wine
Generous ½ cup/125 ml cream
7 oz/200 g crabmeat
3 tbsp chives, finely chopped
½ lemon, zest and juice
Salt and white pepper

FOR THE FISH AND THE SAUCE
3 cups/700 ml water
7 fl oz/200 ml white wine
2 shallots, thinly sliced
1 carrot, peeled and thickly sliced
6 parsley stems
Salt and pepper
7 fl oz/200 ml cream
½ lemon, juiced
2 tbsp chives

For the filling, melt the butter in a large skillet over medium heat, add the shallots, and cook about 1 to 2 minutes until softened but not browned. Sprinkle in the flour and stir to coat the shallots about 1 minute. Pour in the wine and the cream. Simmer for 3 to 4 minutes until the sauce has thickened and reduced by about a third.

Remove the pan from the heat and stir in the crabmeat, chives, lemon zest, lemon juice, salt, and pepper. Transfer to a large bowl, cover loosely with plastic wrap, and refrigerate until completely chilled, about 30 minutes to an hour.

For the fish and sauce, pour the water, wine, shallots, carrot, parsley, and salt into a sauté pan with a fitted lid, and simmer over a medium heat for 15 minutes to create the flavored poaching liquid.

Meanwhile, place the sole fillets in a single layer on a work surface and lightly season both sides with salt and white pepper. Divide the chilled crab filling among the fish fillets, spreading it in a thin, even layer along the length of each fillet, leaving about a

½-inch space to the edge of each fillet. Roll the fillet around the crab stuffing.

Place the rolled fillets seam side down in the poaching liquid in the sauté pan and cover the pan. Poach at a low simmer until the fish is opaque and firm to the touch, about 12 to 15 minutes.

Then, carefully transfer the fish to a warm dish and cover with foil. Bring the liquid remaining in the sauté pan to a boil and reduce to about 3½ fl oz/100 ml; then add the cream and simmer for 2 minutes, whisking occasionally, until the sauce coats the back of a spoon.

Remove the pan from the heat and stir in the lemon juice and chives; season with salt and pepper. Place the paupiettes in a serving bowl and add the sliced carrots.

Serve the paupiettes warm with some fresh parsley stems and a drizzle of sauce.

Serves 6 as a starter/appetizer.

Victoria Sponge with Strawberries

This is one of my favorite classic desserts, and if you are entertaining, this cake will be a treat.

FOR THE SPONGE
3 cups/300 g plain flour
2 tsp baking powder
1½ cups/300 g butter
1½ cups/300 g superfine sugar
5 large eggs
1 tsp vanilla extract

FOR THE FILLING AND TOPPING
6 tbsp strawberry jam
3½ fl oz/110 ml whipped cream
About 20 large/300 g strawberries, sliced
Confectioners' sugar to dust top

Preheat the oven to 350°F/180°C/Gas Mark 4.

Grease two 8 inch/20 cm cake pans and line the bottom of the pans with a round of parchment paper.

In a small bowl, combine the flour with the baking powder.

In a large mixing bowl, beat the butter with the sugar until creamy and fluffy. Then add the eggs, the flour, and vanilla extract.

Transfer evenly to the two prepared cake pans. Bake for 25 to 30 minutes or until a skewer inserted in the center comes out clean. Remove from the oven and transfer to a wire rack to cool.

For the filling, spread some of the strawberry jam on both sponges. Layer the bottom cake with freshly whipped cream and sliced strawberries. Add the second cake with the strawberry jam side down facing the whipped cream. Then, dust the top of the cake with some confectioners' sugar and decorate with sliced strawberries.

Serves 4 to 6

NOTE: Instead of strawberry jam, spread with some berry compote. For alternate fillings use mascarpone and flavored crème fraîche; strawberry purée and mascarpone; flavored and colored butter cream.

Lobster Buttered Soup

2 lobsters (approximate weight 1 lb/450 g each)
¾ lb/300 g mussels
5 fl oz/150 ml white wine

FOR THE FROTH
5 fl oz/150 ml skimmed milk
1 tbsp honey
1 egg
Pinch of salt

FOR THE BROTH
3½ fl oz/100 ml mussel liquid
2 fl oz/50 ml double cream
11 tbsp butter, cubed
1 tbsp lemon juice

Poach the lobsters in a large pot of boiling water for 10 to 12 minutes, then remove from the liquid and crack the shell to remove the meat.

Preheat a pan until smoking hot. Add the mussels and white wine immediately. Cover and cook for 2 to 3 minutes until the shells are open, discardng any that are unopened.

Remove the mussels from the liquid using a slotted spoon. Retain 3½ fl oz/100 ml of liquid to use in the broth. Remove the mussels from their shells, or leave in the shells if you please, and set aside to keep warm.

In the meantime, prepare the froth by just warming to 125°F/60°C the milk, salt, and honey in a saucepan. Remove the saucepan from the heat and add the egg. Without delay, using a hand blender, mix to create the froth. Keep aside warm until needed.

Now prepare the broth. In a small saucepan, bring 3½ fl oz/100 ml of the retained mussel liquid and the cream to a simmer. Whisk in the cubed butter until it creates a smooth buttered broth. Add the lemon juice if needed.

Place the lobster pieces and mussels in 4 shallow serving dishes and add the broth. Froth the milk and spoon over the lobster broth.

Enjoy immediately.

Serves 4

Chicken Ballotines with Potato Farls

A ballotine is a poached parcel of meat usually made with chicken or duck stuffed with juicy filling, then fried to crisp it up!

2 boneless chicken breasts, diced
½ cup/100 g Irish quark cheese (or ricotta)
3 tbsp fresh sage
1 egg white
5 cloves garlic, lightly crushed
2 tbsp chives
Salt and pepper
4 large chicken thighs with skin, deboned
Generous 2 cups/500 ml chicken stock
2 sprigs fresh thyme
8 tbsp butter, cubed
3 tbsp sunflower oil

NOTE: The word *farls* comes from *fardel*, or four parts. It is a flat round of potato bread cut into quarters. Farls are a traditional Northern Ireland dish, especially part of the Ulster fry.

To make the filling/mousse: Place the diced chicken breasts only into a food processor and pulse until smooth. Add the quark (or ricotta), sage, egg white, 3 cloves garlic, chives, and a pinch of salt and pepper and pulse to combine. Transfer the mixture to a piping bag and refrigerate for 1 hour until firm.

Working with one chicken thigh at a time, place between two sheets of plastic wrap and then, using a rolling pin, flatten to an even thickness. Lay out another large sheet of plastic wrap and lay the flattened chicken thigh skin side down in the middle of the film. Season with salt and pepper and then pipe a quarter of the chicken mousse along the center of the meat. Using the plastic wrap to help, roll the chicken up tightly to enclose the filling and create a sausage shape. Tie the ends tightly together to seal. Repeat with the remaining chicken thighs and mousse.

NOTE: Sauté a few small, halved onions to serve with the ballotines, if you like.

Bring a large pan of water to a boil, carefully add the chicken parcels, cover, and simmer on a low heat for 15 minutes. Remove the pan from the heat and allow the chicken to finish poaching in the pan, off the heat, for about 10 to 15 more minutes. With a slotted spoon remove the chicken parcels from the pan, drain on paper towels and leave to cool slightly. Remove from the plastic wrap and pat dry with a kitchen towel.

Meanwhile, place the chicken stock, remaining garlic, a few fresh leaves of sage and thyme in a small saucepan, bring to a boil and boil rapidly until the liquid is reduced by two thirds. Remove the thyme and garlic and whisk in 2 oz/50 g of butter, until well combined.

Just before serving, heat a large nonstick pan over medium/low heat with 2 oz/50 g butter and add the chicken ballotine. Pan fry for about 3 to 5 minutes until the skin is crisp and golden. Season well.

POTATO FARLS

1½ cups/280 g warm mashed potato
Salt and pepper
4 tbsp butter, plus extra for browning farls
¾ cup/85 g plain flour, plus extra for dusting
2 tbsp sage, chopped

Place the mashed potato into a large bowl and season with the salt and black pepper. Melt the butter and add to the potato, then sift in the flour and mix well to make a pliable dough.

Lightly dust your work surface with a little flour, then turn the potato dough onto it and roll into a circle that is roughly ½ inch/1cm thick and 9½ inches/25 cm in diameter. Now divide it into 4 triangles (farls).

Meanwhile, heat a large, heavy-based nonstick frying pan or griddle over a moderate heat. Add extra butter and place the farls to lightly brown. Sprinkle with salt, pepper, and sage. Cook for 2 to 3 minutes on each side until warmed.

For a crispy outside add the farls to the pan of chicken ballotines and panfry with them for 3 to 5 minutes for a crispy surface.

Arrange the ballotines on warm serving plates with the potato farls and spoon over the sauce to serve. Garnish with fresh herbs.

Serves 4

Wexford Berries with Mini Meringues

FOR THE JELLY BASE
17 fl oz/500 ml blackcurrant and apple juice
1 lime, juiced
1 envelope gelatin powder

FOR THE MINI MERINGUES
3 large eggs, whites only
1 cup/220 g superfine sugar
¼ tsp cornstarch
½ tsp vanilla extract

TO DECORATE THE PLATES
7 oz/200 g strawberries, washed and hulled
7 oz/200 g raspberries
2 oz/50 g blueberries
Fresh mint, borage, or basil to decorate

Preheat the oven to 250°F/120°C/Gas Mark ½.

Soak the gelatin in ¼ cup of cold water for about 10 minutes to soften. Pour the apple and blackcurrant juice into a small pan and add the lime juice and softened gelatin. Bring the juice to a gentle simmer whisking continuously for 2 minutes. Remove from the heat.

For the jelly base: Divide the jelly liquid between the serving plates, retaining 3½ fl oz/100 ml to set separately. Add a few strawberries and blueberries to the jelly liquid on the serving plates, and put in the refrigerator to set. Put the separate 3½ fl oz/100 ml of the jelly liquid in a small bowl and into the refrigerator. Let both set for at least 1 hour.

For the mini meringues: Line a baking tray with parchment paper. In a spotlessly clean bowl, whisk the egg white until foamy then add the vanilla and the superfine sugar a little at a time whisking until soft peaks form.

Place in a piping bag mounted with a small star-shape nozzle and pipe small amounts of meringue, about the size of a raspberry, onto the parchment-lined baking tray.

Place in the oven for 10 to 15 minutes until the outside is crunchy and the inside is soft and chewy. Remove from the oven and let cool.

Remove the small bowl from the fridge and whisk the set jelly vigorously until smooth to create the coulis.

When ready to serve place some extra berries and the coulis onto the jelly. Add a few mini meringues and edible flowers or fresh mint.

Serves 4

Scallops and Caviar with Nasturtium Coulis

2 handfuls fresh nasturtium leaves
2 tbsp of mashed potato
2 tbsp cream
3 tbsp water
Salt and pepper
4 large scallops
2 tbsp olive oil
5 fl oz/150 ml milk
1 tsp lemon zest
1 tbsp honey
1 egg
4 tbsp butter
2 tsp caviar
Microgreens for garnish

Prepare the nasturtium coulis. Bring to boil a saucepan of water and prepare aside a bowl of water with ice. Plunge the nasturtium leaves in the boiling water for 10 seconds, remove immediately and plunge them into the iced water. In a second pan, warm the mashed potato with the cream and water. When the potato is of a lighter consistency transfer to a blender and add the nasturtium leaves. Blend until very smooth. Add a squeeze of lemon and pepper. Keep aside warm.

Rub the scallops with olive oil and set aside for a few minutes.

In another saucepan, heat the milk, lemon zest, and honey until about 140°F/60°C. Add the egg to the warm milk and blend with a hand blender to create foam. Remove from the heat.

Sear the scallops in a non-stick pan over very high heat for 1 minute on each side. Reduce the heat to medium, add the butter and continue coating the scallops for 30 seconds. Remove the scallops to some paper towels to remove excess oil, and keep warm.

Blend the milk foam and start plating.

In each serving dish, place a spoon of nasturtium coulis, then the scallop. Top the scallop with caviar and some microgreens. Blend the foam again and spoon over the scallops.

Serves 4

Slow-Cooked Shoulder of Pork with Stuffing, Sautéed Potatoes, and Apple Compote

NOTE: We used ale from Arthurstown Brewing Company in Co. Wexford, a local artisan craft beer brewery using the best locally grown ingredients.

3½ lb/1.5 kg pork shoulder, skin on
1 tbsp sunflower oil
Salt and black pepper
2 carrots, diced
8 cloves garlic, crushed
2 lemons, rind and sliced
20 fl oz/600 ml red ale beer

Preheat the oven to 400°F/200°C/Gas Mark 6.

Score the pork rind and brush with some oil. Rub salt onto the rind. Place the carrots, garlic, and lemon slices into a large roasting pan, and pour the beer over the vegetables. Place the joint of pork onto the vegetables and put in the preheated oven for 30 minutes; then cover with foil, reduce the heat to 300°F/150°C/Gas Mark 2, and cook for a further 2½ to 3 hours. Remove the foil and leave the pork in the oven until the skin is crackling. Remove the pork from the oven and allow to rest on a board for approximately 20 minutes.

NOTE: If you are using dried breadcrumbs you would need 2 cups plus 2 tbsp.

TRADITIONAL STUFFING
10 tbsp + 2 tsp butter
1 large onion, finely chopped
5 cups/250 g fresh white breadcrumbs
1 tbsp chopped sage
1 tbsp fresh thyme
4 tbsp chopped fresh flat-leaf parsley

Preheat the oven to 350°F/180°C/Gas Mark 4.

To make the stuffing, melt the butter in a large skillet and add the onion. Sauté the onion for 3 to 4 minutes until softened and translucent, but not browned. Remove from the heat.

In the meantime, add the breadcrumbs and herbs to a large oven-proof bowl, and mix well. Season to taste. Pour the heated butter and onion over the breadcrumb and herb mixture and place in the preheated oven for 20 to 25 minutes until golden.

SAUTÉED POTATOES
1¼ lb/500 g baby potatoes, peeled
2 tbsp butter
2 onions, finely sliced
Salt and pepper

Place the potatoes in a large pan of salted water and bring to a boil. Lower the heat and simmer for 20 minutes until softened. Remove from the heat and slice into 2 inch/5mm thick slices.

Meanwhile, melt the butter in a large pan over medium heat. Add the onion and cook slowly for 5 minutes covered with a lid until softened. Then, remove the lid, add the potato slices and cook for 6 to 7 minutes. Season to taste.

APPLE COMPOTE
1 to 2 shallots, sliced
2 Granny Smith apples, peeled, cored, and cut into small chunks
5 fl oz/150 ml apple cider
4 tbsp butter
¼ cup/50 g brown sugar
½ cup/100 g sultanas or raisins
Salt and pepper

Take 2 tablespoons of cooking fat from the roasting pan and place in a small saucepan, add the shallots, and cook over a medium heat for 2 to 3 minutes. Add the remaining ingredients and bring to a boil. Reduce the heat and cook until thickened.

Serves 4 to 6

Buttermilk and Heather-Infused Panna Cotta

Panna cotta is an Italian dessert that is very simple to make at home by simmering together cream, milk, and sugar or honey, mixing this with gelatin, and letting it cool until it sets. You can just use vanilla, or some seasonal fruits if you prefer!

5 fl oz/150 ml double cream
4 tbsp comeragh (or any clear) honey
Lavender or heather flowers tied in cheesecloth
10 fl oz/300 ml buttermilk
2 leaves gelatine or ½ envelope powdered gelatin
Raspberries to serve

Place the gelatine leaves in a bowl of water until soft, then squeeze dry (or soak the gelatin powder in ¼ cup of cold water for about 10 minutes to soften).

View of Hook Peninsula from Dunmore East.

Place the cream and honey and the bag of heather in a saucepan over medium heat and stir to dissolve the sugar. Bring to a simmer and remove from the heat. Set aside for 5 minutes to let the flowers infuse the cream mixture. Then remove and discard the cheesecloth sack with the flowers.

Add the softened leaves or the softened powdered gelatin to the warm mixture and stir to dissolve. Add the buttermilk and mix well.

Pour the mixture into 4 glasses or dessert bowls and refrigerate for 3 hours or until set.

Serve with fresh raspberries and a scattering of heather petals.

Serves 4

Munster

Counties: Clare, Cork, Kerry, Limerick, Tipperary, Waterford

Munster is the largest of Ireland's four provinces, with a population of over a million, and comprising counties Clare, Cork, Kerry, Limerick, Tipperary and Waterford. Of these, only Tipperary is landlocked. The others make up a formidable coastline stretching from Waterford in the southeast to Clare in the West. The main towns of the province are located on three of its most important rivers, Limerick on the Shannon, Waterford on the Suir (which partially borders Leinster) and Cork on the Lee. The latter two, together with the Munster Blackwater river, flow from west to east, their valleys following the folds of the adjoining hills. There are, however, higher mountains in Tipperary, and also in Kerry which, in Carrantuohill, can boast of having Ireland's tallest peak. Facing south-west out into the Atlantic, the province gets a goodly share of rain, but also delights in the effects of the Gulf Stream running

along the west coast of the island and bringing a subtropical climate to west Cork and Kerry. The western European *Arbutus*, or wild strawberry, luxuriates in Killarney. The geology is largely carboniferous sandstone and limestone. The lunar-like limestone karst of the Burren at the northern tip of the province in County Clare, provides a most unusual exposure where alpine and arctic flora flourish happily side by side.

The rolling hills and dales of Munster provide lush pasture for the rearing of cattle, so important for the cheese and beef industries, though sheep—for lamb and Irish stew—are plentiful particularly in the hilly regions of Kerry. More unusual are the herds of deer, for venison, around the scenic lakes of Killarney. Abundant fish from the sea and rivers are prized. The climate is favorable for the cultivation of wheat and barley in County Cork, now the home of Ireland's largest whiskey distillery in Midleton.

—Peter Harbison

ABOVE: The Rock of Cashel rising dramatically from the "Golden Vale" in Co. Tipperary is an iconic medieval structure. It is said that here St. Patrick baptised the Munster king, Aengus.

LEFT: The Cliffs of Moher in Co. Clare are the most visited public spot in Ireland. A series of dramatic headlands undulating one behind the other along an eight-mile stretch of Atlantic Ocean coast reach 700 feet above the ocean. From the cliffs on a clear day, one can see the Aran Islands, Galway Bay, and the Twelve Bens—a Connemara mountain range.

Ballymaloe Cookery School
Shannagary
Co. Cork
Chef: Darina Allen

ABOVE: A natural still-life at Ballymaloe.

BELOW: Entrance to the Ballymaloe Cookery School in Shannagary, Co. Cork.

Dubbed "The Julia Child of Ireland" by the *San Francisco Chronicle*, Darina Allen is Ireland's best known cook; a best-selling, award-winning author of many books; pioneer of the slow food movement in Ireland; frequent television guest and presenter; lecturer and teacher. She is a champion of local food sourcing. After working with Myrtle Allen at the famed Ballymaloe House for many years, Darina Allen established the world-renowned Ballymaloe Cookery School at Shannagary in 1983 with her brother Rory O'Connell. The award-winning cookery school sits on its own 100-acre organic farm and gardens, supplying the school with its own all-natural produce.

MENUS

LUNCH

Warm Salad of Gubbeen Bacon with
Poached Egg and Coolea Cheese

Smoked Salmon with Cucumber Pickle

TEA

Florence Bowe's Crumpets

DINNER ONE

Ballycotton Shrimp with
Homemade Wild Garlic Mayonnaise

Ballymaloe Brown Yeast Bread

Roast Lamb with Mint Sauce and Glazed Carrots

Carrageen Moss Pudding

DINNER TWO

Carpaccio of Scallops with Chili, Lemon,
and Wood Sorrel

Poached Salmon with Irish Butter Sauce

Spring Rhubarb Tart with Crystallized Ginger Cream

ABOVE: Darina Allen, the heart and soul of Ballymaloe Cookery School.

LEFT: Students in the Herb Garden at Ballymaloe Cookery School.

Warm Salad of Gubbeen Bacon with Poached Egg and Coolea Cheese

A gorgeous little salad which totally depends on good ingredients. Make it with battery produced eggs and indifferent bacon and you'll wonder why you bothered. If you can't get Gubbeen bacon, look for the best quality smoked bacon you can find.

Caesar Salad Dressing (recipe opposite)
Mixture of fresh salad leaves
6 oz/175 g smoked Gubbeen bacon lardons
A little olive or sunflower oil
4 eggs
2 tbsp fresh grated Coolea cheese, alternatively
    use Parmigiano-Reggiano
Freshly chopped parsley

First make the Caesar dressing: you will have more than you need for this recipe but it keeps for several weeks, so save it in the refrigerator for another time.

Fill a small saucepan with cold water and add a little salt. When the water is boiling, reduce the heat so the water is barely simmering. Crack the egg and allow it to drop gently into the water to cook for 4 to 5 minutes or until the white is set and the yolk is still soft. You may cook the eggs separately or together depending on the size of your saucepan.

Meanwhile heat a frying pan with a little olive or sunflower oil. Cook the lardons of bacon until crispy and golden.

To assemble the salad, put a little Caesar dressing on each plate. Quickly arrange a selection of salad leaves on top. Sprinkle the hot sizzling bacon over the salad, top with a poached egg. Drizzle some Caesar dressing over the poached egg and salad leaves.

Sprinkle with freshly grated or thin slices of cheese and a little chopped parsley. Serve immediately.

Serves 4

Hens roam freely in the Ballymaloe garden.

NOTE: Gubbeen bacon is cured and smoked by a brilliant young artisanal producer called Fingal Ferguson, son of Tom and Giana Ferguson, who make the famous Gubbeen farmhouse cheese on their farm in west Cork.

NOTE: Coolea cheese is a rich and nutty Gouda-type cheese with a glorious waxed rind; it's made from unpasteurized milk by Dick and Helene Williams on their farm in west Cork.

CAESAR DRESSING

2 oz/50 g can anchovies
2 egg yolks, preferably free-range
1 clove garlic, crushed
2½ tbsp lemon juice, freshly squeezed
Generous pinch of English mustard powder
½ tsp salt
½–1 tbsp Worcestershire® sauce
½–1 tbsp Tabasco® sauce
¾ cup/175 ml sunflower oil
¼ cup/50 ml extra-virgin olive oil
¼ cup/50 ml cold water

We make this dressing in a food processor but it can also be made very quickly by hand. Drain the anchovies and crush lightly with a fork. Put into a bowl with the egg yolks, add the garlic, lemon juice, mustard powder, salt, Worcestershire, and Tabasco sauce. Whisk all the ingredients together. As you whisk, add the oils slowly at first, then a little faster as the emulsion forms. Finally whisk in the water. Taste and correct the seasoning; this dressing should be highly flavored.

NOTE: We also add a little freshly cooked asparagus or chicory in season or some chard or beet greens.

Gubbeen Farm
Schull, Co. Cork

ABOVE: Clovisse Ferguson with a basket of lovely organic tomatoes fresh from her Gubbeen Farm garden.

ABOVE, RIGHT: The one fine artisan cheese made at Gubbeen Farm since the 1970s carries the name Gubbeen.

Tom and Giana Ferguson (herdsman and cheesemaker), their son Fingal (the charcutier), and daughter Clovisse (a bio-dynamic gardener) are the extraordinary artisan food producers of Gubbeen Farm, their 250-acre coastal farm in West Cork near the fishing village of Schull in Co. Cork, with the Atlantic Ocean on one side and a sheltering mountain on another. They produce artisan cheese, bacon and smoked meats, and chemical-free vegetables, herbs, fruits, and flowers.

The farm, the garden, and the smokehouse form a strong chain. The progression is perfect: the temperate climate provides the grass for the cows whose milk produces the cheese. The pigs feed on whey—a by-product of the cheese—and the pigs, along with the garden herbs, are central to the cured meat and sausages produced at the smokehouse.

The Ferguson's aim is to reflect in their products what they gain from living in an organic (chemical-free) and seasonal environment.

ABOVE: A range of cured and smoked meats, ham, bacon, sausages, and salamis from Fingal's smokehouse.

LEFT: The full cycle of products from the Gubbeen Farm, from grass to milk to cheese to cured/smoked pork to vegetables and herbs to fresh laid eggs.

Smoked Salmon with Cucumber Pickle

8–10 slices smoked salmon
2 tbsp (or more as you like) Cucumber Pickle (recipe below)
Freshly ground pepper

CUCUMBER PICKLE

This recipe provides 10 to 12 servings, but it keeps well for up to a week in the refrigerator.

6 cups/1 kg thinly sliced unpeeled cucumber
3 small onions thinly sliced
1 cup/225 g sugar
Generous 1 tbsp salt
1 cup/240 ml cider vinegar

Combine the sliced cucumber and onion in a large bowl. Mix the sugar, salt, and vinegar together and pour over cucumbers. Place in a tightly covered container in refrigerator and leave for at least 4 to 5 hours or overnight before using.

Place the sliced salmon and pickled cucumbers on a plate, with a small bowl of homemade mayonnaise (see recipe on p. 94). Garnish with chervil or parsley and wild garlic flowers.

For a special presentation, arrange the pickled cucumbers in a circle on a serving plate. Arrange the salmon slices in a rose shape and place in the center of the cucumber circle.

Serve with homemade mayonnaise and slices of Ballymaloe Brown Yeast Bread (see recipe on p. 95).

Serves 4

Florence Bowe's Crumpets

Another great standby, crumpets can be made in minutes with ingredients you'd probably have on hand. They are also the ideal solution if you've got nothing to serve when a friend drops in for tea, because they only take a few minutes to make. The problem is one always eats too many!

1 ¾ cups/225 g white flour
¼ tsp salt
½ tsp baking powder
1 tsp cream of tartar
2 eggs, preferably free range
1 cup/240 ml milk
Scant ¼ cup/50 g superfine sugar
4 tbsp butter

Sift the dry ingredients into a bowl and rub in the butter. Drop the eggs into the center, add a little of the milk and stir rapidly with a whisk allowing the flour mix to drop gradually in from the sides. When half the milk is added, beat until air bubbles rise. Add the remainder of the milk and allow to stand for one hour if possible. Drop a good (2 teaspoons) dessertspoonful into a medium hot pan and cook until bubbles appear on the top. It usually takes a bit of trial and error to get the temperature right. Flip over and cook until golden on the other side. Serve immediately with butter and home-made jam or, better still, apple jelly. Crumpets can also be served with warm lemon juice and sprinkled with superfine sugar.

Makes approximately 15

NOTE: The crumpets are usually lighter if the batter is allowed to stand, but I've often cooked them immediately with very acceptable results!

RASPBERRY JAM
2 lbs/900 g fresh raspberries
3½ cups/790 g granulated sugar

Preheat the oven to 350°F/180°C/Gas Mark 4.

Wash, dry, and sterilize the jam jars in the preheated oven for 15 minutes. Heat the sugar in the oven for 5 to 10 minutes. Put the raspberries into a wide stainless steel saucepan and cook for 3 to 4 minutes until the juice begins to run, then add the warm sugar and stir over a gentle heat until fully dissolved. Increase the heat and boil steadily for about 5 minutes, stirring frequently.

Raspberry jam is the easiest and quickest of all jams to make, and one of the most delicious. Loganberries, boysenberries, or tayberries may also be used in this recipe.

Hide the jam in a cool place or else put on a shelf in your kitchen so you can feel great every time you look at it! Anyway, it will be so delicious it won't last long!

Test for a set by putting about a teaspoon of jam on a cold plate, leaving it for a few minutes in a cool place. It should wrinkle when pressed with a finger. Remove from the heat immediately. Skim and pour into sterilized jam jars. Cover immediately.

Makes three
2-cup/450g jars

CRAB APPLE OR BRAMLEY APPLE JELLY

6 lb/2.7kg crab apples or windfall cooking apples
11¾ cups/2.7 liter water
2 unwaxed lemons
Sugar as needed

Wash the apples and cut into quarters; do not remove either peel or core. Cut out any bruised parts. Put the apples into a large saucepan with the water and the thinly pared rind of the lemons; cook gently until reduced to a pulp, approximately ¾ hour.

Serve with homemade jam or apple jelly or lemon juice and superfine sugar.

Turn the pulp into a jelly bag and allow to drip into a bowl until all the juice has been extracted, usually overnight. Measure the juice into a preserving pan. Warm a scant 2 cups (15 oz)/ 425 g sugar to each 2½ cups/600 ml of juice in a low oven.

Squeeze the lemons, strain the juice, and add to the preserving pan. Bring to the boil and add the warm sugar. Stir over a gentle heat until the sugar is dissolved. Increase the heat and boil rapidly uncovered without stirring for about 8 to 10 minutes. Skim, test, and pour into jars immediately.

Makes 6 to 7 lb/2.7-3 kg

FOR APPLE AND SWEET GERANIUM JELLY

Add 6 to 8 large leaves of sweet geranium while the apples are stewing and put a fresh leaf into each jar as you add the jelly.

Ballycotton Shrimp with Homemade Wild Garlic Mayonnaise

We get the most wonderful juicy shrimp from the boats in Ballycotton. We eat them in several ways but they are best freshly cooked and served with homemade Wild Garlic Mayonnaise and some crusty bread.

36–40 very fresh shrimp
10 cups/2.3 liters water
2½ tbsp salt

5–10 tbsp homemade Wild Garlic Mayonnaise (recipe follows)

Wild watercress leaves or wood sorrel and 4 segments lemon, for garnish

Bring 10 cups/2.3 liters of water to a boil, add 2½ tablespoons of salt, toss in the live or very fresh shrimp; they will change color from grey to pink almost instantly. Bring the water back to a boil and cook for just 2 to 3 minutes. The shrimp are cooked when there is no trace of black at the back of the head. Drain immediately, and spread out on a large baking tray to cool.

When cold, put 9 to 10 cooked whole shrimp on each plate. Spoon a tablespoon or two of homemade Wild Garlic Mayonnaise (recipe follows) into a little bowl or oyster shell and place on the side of the plate. Add a segment of lemon on the plate, if you like. Alternatively, peel all the shrimp first and then serve or use for another recipe.

Garnish with some fresh wild watercress or wood sorrel. Serve with fresh crusty brown bread.

Serves 4

NOTE: If you wish to serve shrimp without the peel, first remove the head, pinch the end of the tail and tug it, it will pull off half the shell. Remove the remainder of the shell with your fingers. Shrimp are much easier on the fingers than Dublin Bay prawns!

Mayonnaise

Mayonnaise is what we call a "mother sauce" in culinary jargon. In fact, it is the "mother" of all the cold emulsion sauces, so once you can make a mayonnaise you can make any of the daughter sauces by just adding some extra ingredients.

NOTE: Keep the egg whites to make meringues.

NOTE: We use 6 fl oz (¾ cup)/ 175 ml sunflower oil to 2 fl oz (¼ cup)/50 ml olive oil. Alternatively use a ratio of 7 to 1.

Tempting as it may be to reach for the jar of "well-known brand," mayonnaise can be made, even with a hand whisk, in under five minutes; if you use a food processor, it takes even less time. The great secret is to have all your ingredients at room temperature and to drip the oil very slowly into the egg yolks at the beginning. The quality of your mayonnaise will depend totally on the quality of your egg yolks, oil, and vinegar, and it's perfectly possible to make a bland mayonnaise if you use poor quality ingredients.

2 egg yolks, preferably free range
¼ tsp salt
Pinch of English mustard or ¼ tsp French mustard
2 tsp (1 dessertspoon) white-wine vinegar
1 cup/240 ml oil (olive oil, peanut, or sunflower or a mixture)

Put the egg yolks into a bowl with the salt, mustard, and the white-wine vinegar. Put the oil into a measuring cup. With a whisk in one hand and the oil in the other, drip the oil into the egg yolks, drop by drop, whisking at the same time. Within a minute you will notice that the mixture is beginning to thicken. When this happens you can add the oil a little faster, but don't get too cheeky or it will suddenly curdle because the egg yolks can only absorb the oil at a certain pace. Taste and add a little more seasoning and vinegar if necessary.

If the mayonnaise curdles it will suddenly become quite thin, and if left sitting the oil will start to float to the top of the sauce. If this happens you can quite easily rectify the situation by putting another egg yolk or 1 to 2 tablespoons of boiling water into a clean bowl, then whisk in the curdled mayonnaise, a half teaspoon at a time until it emulsifies again.

Serve with cold cooked meats, fowl, fish, eggs, and vegetables.

WILD GARLIC MAYONNAISE
Add 2 to 3 tablespoons plus 2 to 3 teaspoons of freshly chopped wild garlic and 2 to 3 teaspoons of chopped fresh parsley to the above homemade mayonnaise.

Makes 1½ cups

Ballymaloe
Brown Yeast Bread

3½ cups/400 g strong (stone-ground) whole-wheat flour
    plus ½ cup/50 g strong white flour
1 tsp salt
1 tsp black treacle or molasses
Scant 2 cups/425 ml lukewarm water
¾ oz–1oz/20 g–30 g fresh non-GMO yeast
Sesame seeds, optional
1 loaf pan 5 x 8 inch (approximately 13 x 20 cm)
Sunflower oil

Preheat the oven to 450°F/230°C/Gas Mark 8.

Mix the flour with the salt. The ingredients should all be at room temperature. In a small bowl, mix the treacle with some of the water, 5 fl oz (generous ½ cup)/150 ml for 1 loaf, and crumble in the yeast. Let the bowl rest for a few minutes in a warm place to allow the yeast to start to work. Check periodically to see if the yeast is rising. After about 4 or 5 minutes it will have a creamy and slightly frothy appearance on top.

When ready, stir and pour it, with all the remaining water (10 fl oz/275 ml), into the flour to make a loose-wet dough. The mixture should be too wet to knead. Allow to sit in the bowl for 7 to10 minutes (time varies depending on room temperature). Meanwhile, brush the base and sides of the bread pan with a good sunflower oil. Scoop the mixture into the greased pan. Sprinkle the top of the loaves with sesame seeds, if you like. Put the pan in a warm place somewhere close to the stove or near a radiator perhaps. Cover the pan with a tea towel to prevent a skin from forming. Just as the bread comes to the top of the pan, remove the tea towel and put the loaves in the preheated oven for 20 minutes, then turn the oven down to 400°F/200°C/Gas Mark 6 for another 40 to 50 minutes, or until it looks nicely browned and sounds hollow when tapped. The bread will rise a little further in the oven. This is called "oven spring." If however the bread rises to the top of the pan before it goes into the oven it will continue to crisp and flow over the edges.

Makes 1 loaf

NOTE: When making Ballymaloe Brown Yeast Bread, remember that yeast is a living organism that requires warmth, moisture, and nourishment. The yeast feeds on the sugar and produces bubbles of carbon dioxide which causes the bread to rise. Heat of over 120°F/50°C will kill yeast. Have the ingredients and equipment at a lukewarm temperature. White or brown sugar, honey golden syrup, treacle, or molasses may be used. Each will give a slightly different flavor to the bread. At Ballymaloe we use treacle. The dough rises more rapidly with 1 oz/30 g yeast than with ¾ oz/25 g yeast.

We use a stone-ground whole-wheat flour. Different flours produce breads of different textures and flavor. The amount of natural moisture in the flour varies according to atmospheric conditions. The quantity of water should be altered accordingly. The main ingredients—whole-grain flour, treacle, and yeast are highly nutritious.

NOTE: Dried yeast may be used instead of baker's yeast. Follow the same method but use only half the amount given for fresh yeast. Allow longer to rise. Fast acting yeast may also be used, but follow the instructions on the packet.

NOTE: We usually remove the loaf from the pan about 10 minutes before the end of cooking and then put it back into the oven to crisp all round, but if you like a softer crust there's no need to do this.

Roast Lamb with Mint Sauce and Glazed Carrots

NOTE: An average weight leg (or shoulder) of lamb 7 to 8 lbs/ 3.3–3.4 kg will serve 8 to 10 people. Allow approximately 6 oz/175g per person.

NOTE: Have the butcher remove the aitch (pelvic) bone from the top of the leg of lamb, so that it will be easier to carve later, then trim the end of the leg. Score the fat lightly.

1 leg of lamb
4–5 garlic gloves, thinly sliced to slivers
2–3 sprigs thyme or rosemary
Salt and freshly ground pepper

FOR THE GRAVY
2½ cups/600 ml homemade lamb or chicken stock
2 tsp freshly chopped thyme and rosemary
Roux (recipe opposite)
4 tbsp butter cut in pieces to swirl in the gravy
Salt and freshly ground pepper

Preheat the oven to 350°F/180°C/Gas Mark 4.

With the tip of a sharp knife score the fat lightly. Sprinkle with salt and pepper. Place the lamb in a roasting pan in the preheated oven for approximately 1¼ hours for rare, 1½ hours for medium, and 1¾ hours for well done. When the lamb is cooked to your taste, remove the joint to a carving dish to rest while you prepare the gravy.

De-grease the juices in the roasting pan, add the stock, bring to a boil, and thicken with a little roux if desired. Just before serving, whisk in a tablespoon or 2 of butter to enrich the gravy; add the freshly chopped thyme and rosemary.

Serve with Mint Sauce (recipe below) and some sprigs of fresh mint and rosemary or parsley.

Serves 8 to 10

ROUX

8 tbsp butter
1 cup/110 g flour

Melt the butter and cook the flour in it for 2 minutes on a low heat, stirring occasionally. Use as desired. Roux can be stored in a cool place and used when needed or it can be made up on the spot if preferred. It will keep at least two weeks in the refrigerator.

MINT SAUCE

2 tbsp/25 g fresh mint, finely chopped
1 tbsp sugar
½ cup/110 ml boiling water
2 tbsp white-wine vinegar or freshly squeezed
    lemon juice

Put the freshly chopped mint and sugar into a sauce boat. Add the boiling water and vinegar or lemon juice. Allow to infuse for 5 to 10 minutes before serving.

Makes about 6 fl oz (¾ cup)/175ml

NOTE: Traditional mint sauce, made with tender young shoots of fresh mint, takes only minutes to make. Real mint sauce is not a bright green jelly but a slightly dull color and watery texture.

GLAZED CARROTS

1 lb/450 g carrots
1 tbsp butter
4½ fl oz (generous ½ cup)/125 ml cold water
Pinch of salt
A good pinch of sugar

Freshly chopped parsley or fresh mint, for garnish

Cut off the carrot tops and tips, scrub, and peel thinly, if necessary. Cut into slices ⅓ inch/7 mm thick, either straight across or at an angle. Leave very young carrots whole. Put them in a saucepan with butter, water, salt, and sugar. Bring to the boil, cover, and cook over a gentle heat until tender, by which time the liquid should have all been absorbed into the carrots; but if not, remove the lid and increase the heat until all the water has evaporated. Taste and correct the seasoning. Shake the saucepan so the carrots become coated with the buttery glaze.

Serve in a hot vegetable dish sprinkled with chopped parsley or fresh mint.

Serves 4 to 6

NOTE: Cut the carrots into the same thickness, so they will cook evenly.

Carrageen Moss Pudding

My favorite way to eat carrageen moss pudding is just with softly whipped cream and some soft brown sugar sprinkled over the top, but it's also lovely with a fruit compote with any of your family's favorite fruits.

2 tsp/7 g cleaned, well-dried carrageen moss (1 semi-closed fistful)
3¾ cups/900 ml whole milk
1 vanilla pod or ½ tsp pure vanilla extract
1 organic egg
1 tbsp superfine sugar
Lightly whipped cream, for garnish

Soak the carrageen in a little bowl of tepid water for 10 minutes. It will swell and increase in size. Strain off the water and put the carrageen into a saucepan with the milk and the vanilla pod, if using. Bring to the boil and simmer very gently, covered, for 20 minutes. At that point—and not before—separate the egg, put the yolk into a bowl, add the sugar and vanilla extract, if using, and whisk together for a few seconds; then pour the milk and carrageen moss through a strainer onto the egg yolk mixture, whisking all the time. By now the carrageen remaining in the strainer will be swollen and exuding jelly. Press as much of this as possible through the strainer and whisk it into the egg and milk mixture. Test in a saucer as one would with gelatin to see if it is set.

Whisk the egg white stiffly and fold or fluff it in gently. It will rise to make a fluffy top.

Serve the pudding chilled with soft brown sugar and the lightly whipped cream, or with a compote of fruit in season.

Serves 6

GREEN GOOSEBERRY COMPOTE
2 lbs/900 g green gooseberries
2 or 3 elderflower heads
2½ cups/600 ml cold water
1¾ cups/400 g sugar

First remove the tops and tails of the gooseberries. Tie 2 or 3 elderflower heads in a little square of muslin, put in a stainless steel or enamelled saucepan, add the sugar and cover with cold water. Bring

NOTE: When I'm driving through country lanes in late May or early June and suddenly spy the elderflower coming into bloom, I know it's time to search on gooseberry bushes for the hard, green fruit, far too under-ripe at that stage to eat raw but wonderful cooked in tarts or fools or in this delicious compote.

NOTE: Elderflowers were not in season when we were photographing this dish. They are a delicious addition to the compote when possible.

slowly to the boil and continue to boil for 2 minutes. Add the gooseberries and simmer just until the fruit bursts. Allow to get cold. Serve in a pretty bowl and decorate with gooseberries. When in season use fresh elderflowers also.

Serves 6 to 8

NOTE: The tart green gooseberries **must actually** burst otherwise the compote of fruit will be too bitter.

Carpaccio of Scallops with Chili, Lemon, and Wood Sorrel

The scallops for this dish need to be spanking fresh so that the sweet, untainted flavor of the fish shines through. You need to season the scallops with a delicate hand, so go carefully, watching where the seasonings land.

6 large scallops, trimmed of their coral
4 pinches of chili (or crushed red pepper) flakes
Zest and juice of 1 lemon
2½ tbsp best quality olive oil
Generous 1 tbsp wood sorrel leaves
Sea salt and freshly ground black pepper

Slice the scallops horizontally into ⅛ inch/3 to 4 mm slices and divide in a single layer between 4 cold plates, allowing 1½ scallops per serving. Season the scallops with a small pinch of chili flakes, sea salt, and freshly ground black pepper. Finely grate some lemon zest over the scallops and squeeze a little lemon juice over each serving. Sprinkle on the wood sorrel leaves and finally drizzle with olive oil. Serve immediately.

Serves 4

NOTE: If wood sorrel isn't available, coriander (cilantro) can be used instead.

NOTE: The scallop coral is not used in this dish as their texture is not entirely suitable for eating raw, but save them for a chowder or a scallop mousse.

Students at work in the Ballymaloe Cookery School kitchen.

Poached Salmon with Irish Butter Sauce

2½ lb/1.1 kg center cut of fresh salmon
Water
Salt

FOR THE IRISH BUTTER SAUCE
2 egg yolks
2 tsp (1 dessertspoon) cold water
8 tbsp butter, diced
Approximately 1 tsp lemon juice

Sprigs of flat parsley or watercress, for garnish

NOTE: For maximum flavor, we cook the salmon in the time-honored way, by poaching it gently in well-salted boiling water. The proportion of salt to water is very important. We use one rounded tablespoon of salt to every 5 cups/1.2 liters of water. The fish or piece of fish should be just covered with water, using the minimum amount of water to preserve the maximum flavor, so one should use a saucepan that will fit the fish exactly. An oval cast-iron saucepan is usually perfect.

Half-fill the pan with measured salted water and bring to a boil. Put in the piece of fish, just covering it with water, and bring back to a boil. Simmer gently, adjusting the heat as necessary, for 20 minutes. Turn off the heat, and allow the fish to sit in the water. Serve within 15 to 20 minutes.

Meanwhile, make the Irish butter sauce. Put the egg yolks into a heavy-bottomed stainless-steel saucepan on a very low heat. Add the cold water and whisk thoroughly.

Add the butter bit by bit, whisking all the time. As soon as one piece melts, add the next. The mixture will gradually thicken, but if it shows signs of becoming too thick or "scrambling" slightly, remove from the heat immediately and add a little cold water if necessary. Do not leave the pan or stop whisking until the sauce is made. Finally add the lemon juice to taste. Pour into a bowl and keep warm over hot, but not boiling, water.

Lift the cooked salmon carefully out of the poaching liquid and place on a platter. Cut the poached salmon into individual servings. Gently peel off the salmon skin. Put a few tablespoons of butter sauce on a plate, add the portion of salmon, and finish with more sauce. Garnish with sprigs of parsley or watercress.

Serves 8

MELTED LEEKS

2 lbs/900 g leeks (once prepared)
4 tbsp butter
2½ tbsp water if necessary
Salt and freshly ground pepper
Chopped parsley or chervil

Cut off the dark green leaves from the top of the leeks. Slit the leeks about half way down the center and wash well under cold running water. Slice into ⅓ inch/5 mm rounds. Melt the butter in a heavy casserole; when it foams, add the sliced leeks and toss gently to coat with butter. Season with salt and freshly ground pepper. Cover with a round of wax paper cut to fit the inside of the pan and a close-fitting lid. Reduce the heat and cook very gently for approximately 8 to 10 minutes, or until semi-soft and moist. Check and stir occasionally. Turn off the heat and allow to continue cooking in the heat. Serve on a warm dish sprinkled with chopped parsley or chervil.

Serves 8 to 10

NOTE: The pot of leeks may be cooked in the oven at 325°F/170°C/Gas Mark 3 if that is more convenient.

Spring Rhubarb Tart with Crystallized Ginger Cream

The pastry is made by the creaming method so people who are convinced that they suffer from "hot hands" don't have to worry about rubbing in the butter.

FOR THE PASTRY
1 cup/225 g butter
Scant ¼ cup/40 g superfine sugar
2 eggs, preferably free range
2¾ cups/300 g white flour, preferably unbleached

FOR THE FILLING
2 lb/900 g red rhubarb, sliced about ½ inch/1cm thick
Generous ¾–1 cup/175–225 g sugar.
Egg wash, made with one beaten egg and a dash of milk
Superfine sugar for sprinkling

FOR SERVING
Softly whipped cream with chopped crystallized ginger or Barbados sugar

Baking pan, 7 inches x 12 inches/18 cm x 30.5cm x 1 inch/ 2.5 cm deep

Preheat the oven to 350°F/180°C/Gas Mark 4.

To make the pastry, cream the butter and sugar together by hand or in a food mixer (no need to overcream). Add the eggs and beat for several minutes. Reduce the speed and mix in the flour. Turn out onto a piece of floured parchment paper, flatten into a round, wrap and chill. This pastry needs to be chilled for at least 2 hours, otherwise it is difficult to handle.

To make the tart, roll out the pastry to approximately ⅛ inch/3 mm thick, and use about ⅔ of it to line a suitable pan. Put the prepared rhubarb into the pan and sprinkle with the sugar. Cover with a lid of pastry, seal edges, decorate with pastry leaves and egg wash; bake in the preheated oven until the rhubarb is tender, approximately 45 minutes to 1 hour. When cooked, cut into squares, sprinkle lightly with superfine sugar, and serve with crystallized ginger whipped cream or Barbados sugar and softly whipped cream.

Serves 8 to 12

English Market in Cork

The bustling English Market in the center of Cork, opened in 1788, is Ireland's most famous covered food market. After a fire destroyed it in 1980, the rebuilt market included a fine restaurant on the upper level. The hard-to-resist stalls offer everything from fresh vegetables, fruit, cheese, bread, meat and fish, and a certified organic market. English Market is also the place that has defined the artisan food movement in Ireland.

Global Village
Dingle
Co. Kerry
Chef: Martin Bealin

Martin Bealin, a Food Ambassador for Tourism Ireland is the chef/owner of Global Village, an award-winning restaurant in the center of Dingle. Martin and Nuala Cassidy opened the restaurant in 1997.

ABOVE: Lettuce leaves from Martin Bealin's garden.

RIGHT: Chef-owner Martin Bealin in the doorway of his award-winning Global Village Restaurant in Dingle.

MENUS

LUNCH

Dingle Bay Scallops, Poached Eggs, Potato Cakes,
and Burnt Butter Hollandaise, with Pickled Cucumber

Goat Cheese Mousse, Beet Chutney,
Caramelized Hazelnuts, and Apple Crisps

DINNER ONE

Trio of Local Brown Crab:
Crab Parfait, Crabmeat and Apple Salad, and Bisque Shot

West Kerry Lamb:
Braised Lamb with Pearl Barley Risotto

Buttermilk Posset with Almond Biscuits

DINNER TWO

Smoked Duck Breast with Duck Liver Pâté and
Sultana and Apple Chutney

Seared Dingle Bay Scallops, Pea Purée, Pork Breast,
and Apple Crisps

Rhubarb Crumble with Salted Caramel Ice Cream

ABOVE: Martin Bealin, founder of the Dingle Food Festival, celebrating its ninth year.

BELOW: Interior of Global Village set for dinner.

Working in several restaurants around the world, Martin brought home a stylish sophistication with dishes created from locally sourced and environmentally sustainable produce. He uses local vegetables from his own bio-dynamic garden, beef and lamb from local farmers (always identified on the blackboard in the restaurant) and fish fresh off the boats in Dingle's quay. He offers several dishes as a duo or trio featuring an imaginative treatment of a single ingredient, like the recipe for the Trio of Brown Crab offered here.

Dingle Bay Scallops, Poached Eggs, Potato Cakes, and Burnt Butter Hollandaise, with Pickled Cucumber

FOR THE CUCUMBER PICKLE
1 cucumber
2 tbsp fresh dill
1½ cups/355 ml cider vinegar
1 cup/225 g sugar
5–6 black peppercorns
¼ teaspoon salt

FOR THE POTATO CAKE
½ white onion, finely diced
2 large potatoes
1 clove crushed garlic
3–4 sprigs thyme
2–3 tbsp vegetable oil
Salt and cracked black pepper

FOR THE POACHED EGGS
4 eggs
2 tsp white wine vinegar

FOR THE HOLLANDAISE
8 tbsp unsalted butter
2 large egg yolks
1½ tbsp hot water
1 tsp white wine
1 tsp white-wine vinegar
Salt and pepper to taste

FOR THE SCALLOPS
8 bay scallops
Oil for cooking
Butter

Preheat oven to 400°F/200°C/Gas Mark 6.

CUCUMBER PICKLE

Cut the cucumbers in half and using a spoon, scoop out and discard the watery flesh on the inside. Finely slice the cucumber halves and set aside. Place all other ingredients in a saucepan and bring to a boil. Lower the heat and allow to simmer for 5 minutes. Pour over the cucumbers while still hot. Allow to cool completely before covering and refrigerating them.

POTATO CAKE

Finely dice the onion and chop the fresh herbs. Then, peel and grate the potatoes; place them in a cloth and squeeze out the excess liquid. Mix all ingredients together and season. Shape into circles, using a cutter if necessary. Lightly brown on both sides in a hot pan with a little oil, and finish in the preheated oven for about 8 to 12 minutes.

POACHED EGGS

Bring a heavy wide-based saucepan of water to the boil. Reduce the heat so that the water is simmering. Add 2 teaspoons of white-wine vinegar. Crack the eggs, one at a time, into a cup. Whisk the water in a circular motion, causing a whirlpool effect, and carefully drop in the eggs one at a time. You can poach all the eggs at the same time, as long as they are added one at a time. The circular motion of the water helps the eggs form a more rounded appearance. Cook for 4 to 6 minutes or until desired texture is reached.

BURNT HOLLANDAISE

Place the butter in a heavy-based saucepan and leave on a medium heat until the butter turns to a nice brown color: it will smell slightly of nuts. Allow to cool. In a large metal bowl, add the egg yolk, vinegar, white wine, and seasoning. Over a low heat whisk the egg mixture briskly and firmly until the mixture forms the figure 8 on top and holds. Take off the heat and very slowly add the browned butter while continuing to whisk. If the mixture becomes too thick or looks to be splitting add a few teaspoons of warm water. Season and taste, and keep in a warm place before using.

SCALLOPS

Remove the roe and any sinew around the scallop. Heat a pan and add a little oil; just before cooking, season the scallops with salt and pepper. Sear on one side for 2 minutes until they are golden, turn over and cook for another minute and a half. Add a small piece of butter and allow to rest for 1 minute before plating the dish.

Build the dish by placing the potato cake in the center of the plate, topped with scallops. Carefully place the poached egg on top and nap with the burnt hollandaise. Garnish the plate with the pickled cucumber and some fresh herbs.

Serves 4

Goat Cheese Mousse, Beet Chutney, Caramelized Hazelnuts, and Apple Crisps

FOR THE BEET CHUTNEY
1.1 pounds/550 g beets,
    without greens, washed
1 onion, finely diced
1 tsp chopped garlic
1 tsp grated fresh ginger
2 tsp ground cardamom
1 tsp ground cloves
1 tsp cumin
1 cup/225 g superfine sugar
1 cup/240 ml cider vinegar
oil for cooking

FOR THE APPLE CRISPS
1 apple
1 cup/225 g sugar
1 cup/240 ml water
1 cinnamon stick

FOR THE MOUSSE
6 oz/170 g good quality goat cheese
3 oz/85 g cream cheese
¼ cup/60 ml cream
1 tsp of honey

FOR THE CARAMELIZED HAZELNUT
1 cup/150 g hazelnuts
2 tsp superfine sugar
1 tbsp water

NOTE: You may also add some fresh herbs, roasted vegetables, or arugula for color.

NOTE: The stock syrup can be stored in the refrigerator, and used to dry any fruit in the same way.

For the beet chutney, put the beets in a saucepan and add enough boiling water to cover them about a half. Cover the pot and cook for ¾ hour to an hour, until they are just falling off a knife when pierced. Large beets will take longer. Strain and allow to cool before peeling and dicing.

In a heavy-based saucepan add a little oil and finely diced onion, garlic, and ginger, allowing to cook until softened. Add the diced beets and mix thoroughly. Add the cardamom, cloves, cumin, sugar, and vinegar bringing slowly to a boil and then reduce to a simmer. Cover and allow to cook until a jam consistency is reached but the beets retain their shape.

For the apple crisps, slice the apples very thin, avoiding the core. Place on a baking pan.

Meanwhile, make a stock syrup by bringing the sugar, water, and cinnamon stick to a boil for about 5 minutes, until the sugar melts. Remove from heat and allow to cool enough to use. Brush the apple slices with the stock syrup and place in a low heat oven 176°F/80°C for 5 to 8 minutes until crisp and golden.

For the goat cheese mousse, combine in a bowl the goat chese, cream cheese, cream, and honey and incorporate well using a spatula. Place in the refrigerator to set for at least 1 hour before using.

Meanwhile, put the hazelnuts on a baking pan and place under the broiler for 1 to 2 minutes. Remove from the oven. Remove the skins by putting the hazelnuts in a cloth and rubbing together: the skin will come off easily. Sprinkle with the superfine sugar and a tablespoon of water and allow to caramelize. Turn out on to a sheet of parchment paper and allow to cool before plating the dish.

To serve, place dollops of the goat cheese mousse onto a plate, garnish with the apple crisps and chutney. Sprinkle with the caramelized hazelnuts.

Serves 4

Trio of Local Brown Crab: Crab Parfait, Crabmeat and Apple Salad, and Bisque Shot

5–6 large fresh, live
    brown crabs

FOR THE CRAB PARFAIT
8 oz/225 g brown crabmeat
Generous 8 tbsp softened butter
1½ sheets gelatin leaves,
    soaked in cold water
3 tbsp port
1 tsp whole-grain mustard
1 tbsp chopped parsley
Cracked black pepper
    to taste

FOR THE CRABMEAT AND APPLE SALAD
10 oz/285 g white crabmeat
1 red apple, finely diced
3–4 tbsp good quality mayonnaise
Freshly chopped dill
Salt and cracked black pepper to taste

FOR THE CRAB BISQUE
4–6 cups crab shells
½ cup/120 ml cognac or whiskey
1 onion, roughly chopped
1 carrot, roughly chopped
2 tbsp tomato paste
2 sprigs thyme
Parsley sprigs and stalks
2 bay leafs
10–15 black peppercorns
20 oz can chopped tomatoes
1–2 cups/240–470 ml water
5 drops of Tabasco sauce

To cook the crabs, put them in a pot of boiling water, cover, and cook for 15 minutes. Remove and allow to cool before further preparation.

Break down the crab by first removing the claws. Using the back of a heavy knife or crab hammer, open the claws and remove all the white meat including the meat in the knuckles. Set aside.

To remove the brown meat from the crab bodies, place them upside down and apply pressure to the belly, pushing upward to open. Be sure to remove the inedible parts—the gills and cartilage; only use the soft brown liquid substance for the parfait.

Carefully go through the crabmeat to remove all traces of shell. Keep all shells for the bisque.

CRAB BISQUE

In a tall heavy-based pot, crush the crab shells with the end of a rolling pin to extract more flavor while the shells are cooking. Cook on a high heat for about 10 minutes and add the whiskey. Allow the alcohol to burn off before adding the remainder of the ingredients. Add the vegetables and herbs, canned tomatoes, tomato paste and enough water to cover the shells. Allow to boil first for a half hour and reduce to simmer for a further hour. Drain the liquid through a very fine strainer to remove all sediment and traces of shell. Pour the liquid into a fresh pot on a low heat to allow the flavor to enhance and the bisque to reduce and thicken. You may use a roux here to thicken. A roux is made with equal quantities of butter and flour made into a paste, added to the bisque and cooked out completely. To finish the bisque add some seasoning and the Tabasco. Taste the bisque throughout the cooking process to regulate the salt content, add only a little salt when seasoning. Keep warm.

CRABMEAT AND APPLE SALAD

Place the crabmeat in a bowl and ensure there is no crab shell in the white meat, going through it little by little with your fingers. To this add a finely diced apple, along with the chopped dill and a good quality mayonnaise. Season lightly and refrigerate until serving.

BROWN CRAB PARFAIT

Make this in a food processor and then cook over a bain marie (double boiler). Place the brown crab meat, softened butter, mustard, black pepper, and herbs in a food processor. Blend the mixture at a high speed for a few minutes and then lower to a medium speed.

Meanwhile, soak the gelatin leaves in some cold water for a few minutes to soften. Once softened, squeeze them to eliminate the water.

In a small saucepan, heat the port and when boiling whisk in the softened gelatin leaves. Add the port mixture to the parfait while continuing to blend. Then strain the mixture through a fine sieve into a metal bowl and cook over a bain marie. Use a thermometer to ensure it reaches a temperature of 200°F/68°C. Scoop the parfait into individual ramekins and cover with clarified butter. Allow to set in the refrigerator for 2 to 3 hours.

To serve, place the ramekin of parfait on the serving plate with a scoop of crab and apple salad. Add a glass of crab bisque. Garnish with fresh greens and herbs and a Seaweed Biscuit, if you wish.

Serves 4

SEAWEED BISCUITS

These biscuits are a perfect accompaniment to this delicious crab trio.

1 cup/110 g white flour
½ cup/120 ml egg white
1 tbsp melted butter
¼ cup/50 g dried chopped
    seaweed (dillisk or kombu)
Salt and cracked black pepper

Preheat the oven to
400°F/200°C/Gas Mark 6.

Whisk together all the ingredients to form a thick batter. Using a spoon, drop some of the mixture onto a silicone baking mat.

Drag the back of the spoon across the mixture to form a flat strip (Tuile).

Bake at preheated oven for 12 minutes until golden and crisp.

West Kerry Lamb: Braised Lamb with Pearl Barley Risotto

NOTE: The meat, fat, and carti-lage between the bones has been removed from a Frenched chop.

NOTE: Arborio rice may be used in place of the pearl barley.

NOTE: In the restaurant we pre-pare this dish with Frenched rib chops, boneless rump sirloin, and breast. This is in the photograph. But you can use any lamb cuts you prefer.

4 Frenched rib chops plus 12 oz/340 g boneless loin
 (or your preferred cut)
2–3 tsp ground cilantro and fennel
Salt and black pepper
Rapeseed oil, for searing
Butter, for reheating

FOR THE PEARL BARLEY RISOTTO
Oil, for sautéeing
2 shallots, finely diced
1 clove garlic, crushed
2 sprigs rosemary, chopped
1 cup/213 g pearl barley
Dash of red wine or port
4 tbsp butter
2 cups/470 ml vegetable stock
Salt and cracked black pepper to taste
Oil

Small whole cooked carrots, for garnish

Preheat oven to 400°F/200°C/Gas Mark 6.

Season the chops well with the ground spices, salt, and pepper. Heat a large pan with a little oil and quickly sear the chops in a hot pan until they are browned on all sides, adding more oil as necessary. Remove from the pan and transfer to a wide pot with the sirloin; place in the oven for 20 minutes for a medium result. Remove from the oven when done and set aside to rest.

Both meats can be cooked in advance and reheated before plating.

For the risotto, sauté the finely diced onion, chopped rosemary, and garlic with some oil in a heavy-based wide pot. Add the pearl barley along with some butter and coat the barley completely with butter. A dash of red wine or port can be added now to deglaze the pan. Little by little add the vegetable stock until the barley is al dente (slightly firm). Finish the barley by adding the remaining butter which gives a rich finish.

Meanwhile add some butter to the top of the meat to add some moisture, and reheat under the broiler.

Put a spoon of the risotto on a plate. Add the lamb with some of the juice from the meats. Decorate with herbs and small, whole cooked carrots.

Serves 4

Buttermilk Posset with Almond Biscuits

Kinsale in Co. Cork is at the southern end of the Wild Atlantic Way on a peninsula jutting out into the Atlantic. It is the home of the world-class Old Head Golf Course.

NOTE: Posset is similar to panna cotta.

FOR THE POSSET
14 fl oz/415 ml cream
7 fl oz/205 ml buttermilk
½ cup/110 g superfine sugar
2 lemons, juice and grated rind

FOR THE ALMOND BISCUITS:
3 large eggs
1 tsp almond extract
½ cup/110 g sugar
3 cups/340 g all-purpose flour
1 tsp baking powder
1¼ cup/170 g toasted almonds, roughly chopped

Strawberries, lemon rind (finely sliced), and confectioners' sugar, for garnish

Preheat the oven to 300°F/150°C/Gas Mark 2.

Place the cream, buttermilk, and sugar in a saucepan and bring slowly to a boil. Remove from the heat as soon as it starts to bubble. Add the lemon juice and some grated rind. Pour into clean molds (ramekins) and allow to cool before setting in the refrigerator for approximately 2 hours to set firmly.

To make the almond biscuits, line a baking sheet with parchment paper. In a small bowl lightly beat the eggs, almond extract, and sugar. Sift together the flour and baking powder. Gradually add the wet mixture to the flour and continue to mix. Add the toasted almonds. The mixture should resemble dough. Shape the dough into a log on a floured surface. Transfer the log to the baking sheet and bake in the preheated oven for 30 minutes. Allow to cool and cut the log into biscuit shapes and bake for a further 10 to 15 minutes. Allow to cool on a wire rack.

To serve, unmold the set posset by dipping the molds into a little hot water and then turning them upside down on a dessert plate. Serve with some candied lemon peel, fresh strawberries, and biscuits dusted with confectioners' sugar.

Serves 4

Smoked Duck Breast with Duck Liver Pâté and Sultana and Apple Chutney

1 large duck breast, smoked

FOR THE PÂTÉ
10 tbsp butter
10 oz/285 g duck liver
¾ cup/180 ml cream
1 tbsp whiskey
2–3 sprigs thyme
Salt and cracked black pepper

FOR THE SULTANA AND APPLE CHUTNEY

1 lb/450 g cooking apples, peeled and cored
1 small onion, diced
Oil for cooking
Scant 1 cup/200 g sultanas, or raisins
Generous 1 cup/225 g firmly packed brown sugar
1 tsp ground ginger
1 tsp salt
1 tsp ground five-spice powder
1 cup/240 ml cider vinegar

The smoked duck can be purchased already prepared. In the restaurant we have a smoking unit in which we use whiskey oak-smoked flavor wood to give the duck breasts a unique flavor. The duck breasts are then lightly salted and placed on wire racks in the smoker for 2 to 3 hours at a low temperature. They are then cooked in the oven for 5 to 8 minutes at 350°F/180°C/Gas Mark 4.

LIVER PÂTÉ

In a heavy-based saucepan melt the butter at a low heat. Add the livers, thyme, and whiskey. Stir lightly and cook until the livers are done all the way through. Cut one with a knife through the middle to ensure this. Add the cream and black pepper. Blend at a medium speed in a food processor until smooth. Put into a small bowl or turn into a prepared pan for setting in the refrigerator. The pâté is best made 3 to 4 hours in advance of serving to set firmly.

APPLE CHUTNEY

Finely dice the apples and the onion. Cook at a medium heat with a little oil until beginning to soften. Add the sultanas or raisins. Then add the remainder of the ingredients and coat the apple mixture thoroughly in all the spices. Bring to a boil and then reduce the heat to a low simmer. Stir the mixture every few minutes to ensure it does not stick. Taste and correct seasoning, if necessary.

Place a scoop of the chutney and pâté on the plate, and then arrange the slices of duck on top, garnished with some fresh greens. The smoked duck is best served warm. In the restaurant we serve this dish with some Melba toast or croutons.

Serves 4

Seared Dingle Bay Scallops, Pea Purée, Pork Breast, and Apple Crisps

FOR THE PEA PURÉE
2 cups/306 g frozen peas
1 cup/240 ml cream
4 tbsp butter

FOR THE APPLE CRISPS
1 red apple
1 cup/225 g sugar
1 cup/240 ml water
1 stick cinnamon

20 oz/560 g pork breast, cut as four 5-oz portions
Fennel seeds
16 scallops
2–3 radishes, sliced wafer thin
Salt and cracked black pepper

Preheat the oven to 200°F/80°C/Gas Mark ¼.

Place the frozen peas, cream, butter, and seasoning in a saucepan and heat until the mixture begins to bubble slightly. Blend the mixture until smooth; remove from the heat and set aside.

APPLE CRISPS
Slice the apple very thinly, avoiding the core. Place on a baking sheet. Make a stock syrup by bringing 1 cup sugar, 1cup water, and cinnamon stick to a boil for 5 minutes. Remove from heat and allow to cool. Brush the apple slices with the stock syrup and place in the preheated heat oven for 5 to 8 minutes until crisp and golden.

PORK BREAST
Preheat oven to 425°F/220°C/Gas Mark 7

Score the fat on the pork with a sharp knife and rub in some salt and fennel seeds. Sear the pork in a hot pan with a little oil, until the skin is crisp, and then place in the preheated oven for 20 minutes. Lower the heat to 300°F/150°C/Gas Mark 2, turn over the meat, and cook for a further 5 minutes. Remove from the heat and allow the meat to rest while the scallops are being cooked.

SCALLOPS

Season the scallops and add to a hot pan with a little oil. Cook for about 2 minutes, until golden. Turn over and cook for a further minute. Add some butter and remove from the heat to allow the scallops to finish cooking in the hot pan.

Heat the pea purée in a small pan and place on a serving plate. Add the pork, scallops, and apple crisps. Garnish with thin radish slices and garden greens.

Serves 4

Rhubarb Crumble with Salted Caramel Ice Cream

FOR THE CRUMBLE
½ cup/110 g superfine sugar
3 tbsp port
1 lb/450 g rhubarb
1½ cups/170 g cake flour
¼ cup/60 g light brown sugar
4 tbsp chilled diced butter
4 tbsp chopped walnuts or almonds

FOR THE ICE CREAM
1 cup/240 ml milk
1 fresh vanilla pod (or 1 tsp vanilla extract)
4 large egg yolks
¾ cup/170 g sugar
2 cups/470 ml heavy cream

FOR THE SALTED CARAMEL
1¼ cups/285 g sugar
¾ cup/180 ml heavy cream
1 tbsp vanilla extract
2 tsp flaked sea salt

Preheat oven to 375°F/190°C/Gas Mark 5.

For the rhubarb crumble, place the superfine sugar and port in a saucepan and leave on a low heat. Wash and chop the rhubarb into a large dice. Then add the chopped rhubarb to the saucepan and stew at a low heat for 10 to 15 minutes, until tender but cooked. In another bowl, mix together the flour, sugar, and butter until the mixture resembles breadcrumbs. Add the chopped nuts. Pour the stewed rhubarb into an ovenproof dish and top generously with the crumble topping. Bake in the preheated oven for 20 minutes until golden on top.

SALTED CARAMEL ICE CREAM

Heat the cream and milk in a saucepan with a split fresh vanilla pod. In a large bowl whisk together the egg yolk and sugar until pale and fluffy (a sabayon). Allow the cream and milk to cool slightly before adding to the sabayon, whisking constantly. Place the ice cream base into a saucepan and heat until the mixture thickens and coats the back of a spoon. Pass through a fine sieve and allow to cool completely before placing in an ice cream churner.

For the salted caramel, put all the ingredients except for the salt in a heavy-based saucepan. The mixture will dissolve and then begin to darken. Remove from the heat when golden as it will burn fast.

Add the sea salt flakes. Allow to cool slightly before adding to the ice cream in the churner.

The crumble is best served warm and topped with the salted caramel ice cream.

Serves 4

NOTE: A good quality store-bought ice cream is a fine option. You could make the salted caramel and pour it over vanilla ice cream or even mix it into the ice cream. Or ice cream alone is fine.

Murphy's Ice Cream
Dingle, Co. Kerry

Imagine! An ice cream handmade with such local natural ingredients that you know where the cows graze—that's the rare black Kerry cow. And it tastes so good you want to know the source. A sign on their shop front (and on their website) reads "Ice cream that knows where it's coming from." And many ice cream fanciers know just where *they* are going! Murphy's Ice Cream in Dingle, an artisan producer of this fine ice cream since 2000. The Murphy brothers—Sean and Kieran—though born in the US made frequent trips to Ireland as children (their father was Irish) and decided to make their way to Dingle.

They collect sea water from the Dingle shore to make their own sea salt, and distill Dingle rain to make their sorbets. With fresh local farm milk from the Kerry cows and cream, free-range eggs, and organic sugar this has to be the best flavored ice cream. And word is that if you offer an idea for a favorite or an interesting flavor, they might just try it. They keep a record of which flavors sell, and those that don't. Some of the creations sound bizarre: There is a Dingle Sea Salt, along with Caramelized Brown Bread, Baked Banana, Blue Cheese and Caramelized Shallot (the weirdest flavor they ever made). Of course, there are all-time favorites like Kerry Cream Vanilla, Chocolate Chip, Nutty Crunch Peanut and others.

How can you resist such imagination and sheer pleasure?

ABOVE: Pulling ice cream from the machine.

ABOVE: A cone of black currant sorbet made with distilled rain water.

RIGHT: Sean and Kieran happily enjoying their own creations.

ABOVE: Collecting a bucket of sea water to make sea salt for the ice cream.

Connacht

Counties: Galway, Leitrim, Mayo, Roscommon, Sligo

RIGHT: Small fishing boats moored in Roundstone harbor in Connemara.

OPPOSITE, TOP: Lough Gill, this graceful, peaceful island-studded lake, is celebrated in William Butler Yeats' poem "The Lake Isle of Innisfree."

OPPOSITE, BOTTOM: The peaceful stillness of Derryclare Lough in Connemara, Galway captured in the soft, diffused end-of-day light.

Connacht is the only one of the four Irish provinces whose name doesn't end in –ster, a corruption of an old Scandinavian word meaning place. Instead, it was called after a rather mythological character named Conn of the Hundred Battles—the number of which have fortunately been reduced over the centuries. Its counties are Galway, Leitrim, Mayo, Roscommon, and Sligo, taking up the western and northwestern sector of the island and (minus Clare, which once belonged to it) occupying the territory west of the river Shannon, the longest river in Britain or Ireland. Together with the midlands east of the Shannon, Connacht has one of the greatest concentrations of peat or turf bog which covered almost one sixth of the surface of Ireland centuries ago, but which has declined within the last three-quarters of a century because of its exploitation for fuel and garden fertilizer. Its

presence in Connacht reduced the amount of arable land, which led to Ireland's ogre Oliver Cromwell punishing many Catholics east of the Shannon in the mid-seventeenth century by ordering them to go "to hell or to Connaught" (the older English spelling of the province).

The western parts of Galway and Mayo, and to a lesser extent Sligo, are quite mountainous, where sheep may graze in multitudes, and provide plentiful lamb for Easter. You can't eat scenery, they say, but you can at least enjoy it here! The very indented coastline favors oyster beds, and small craft do fish for lobster, in the absence of any large-scale commercial marine exploitation. The lesser rivers of Mayo which drain into the Atlantic still have an appreciable amount of salmon and trout for the lucky angler. Sport fishing is also popular in the sizeable Connacht lakes of Conn, Mask, and Corrib, at the southern end of the province. Galway is the provincial capital.

—**Peter Harbison**

LEFT: Storm clouds gather over Keem Strand, Achill Island, at the edge of the Atlantic Ocean in Co. Mayo. The largest island in Ireland, Achill Island connects to the mainland by a bridge.

Ballynahinch Castle
Recess, Connemara
Co. Galway
Chef: Ultan Cooke

Michelin-starred Ultan Cooke is Head Chef at Ballynahinch Castle in Connemara. Ballynahinch, set on a magical 450-acre estate of woodlands and rivers with a famous salmon fishery and a backdrop of the Twelve Bens mountains, is one of Ireland's finest luxury hotels Ultan Cooke's philosophy of using fresh, local, seasonal ingredients is literally naturally supported with the surrounding unspoiled Connemara countryside. Plentiful fish, shellfish, and game available on the west coast provide the base for his imaginative, creative dishes with menus changing regularly to reflect the season. The *Irish Examiner* has said that this was a restaurant to get excited about.

MENUS

LUNCH

**Whipped Goat Cheese with Beet Slaw
and Apple Syrup**

DINNER ONE

Sea Scallops with Puréed and Pickled Cauliflower

Lamb, Samphire, and Burnt Onion Purée

Rose Water Crème Brûlée

DINNER TWO

Wood Pigeon, Gooseberry, and Spinach

Sweaty Betty with Barley and Seaweed

**Sheep Yogurt Mousse
with Marinated Strawberries and Mint**

ABOVE: The dining room of the restaurant at Ballynahinch Castle looking out to the winding river making ts way to the sea through the lush greenery of Connemara. Ballynahinch offers guests the very best fly fishing in Connemara.

OPPOSITE, TOP: Ultan Cooke, Head Chef at Ballynahinch Castle.

OPPOSITE, BOTTOM: The magnificent scenery of Connemara at its best surrounds Ballynahinch Castle overlooking its famous salmon fishery and the Twelve Bens mountains as a backdrop.

Whipped Goat Cheese with Beet Slaw and Apple Syrup

2 lb/900 g creamy goat cheese, allowing about 5 oz/150 g
    per person
¼ cup/50 g crème fraîche

2 cups/410 g beets
7 fl oz/200 ml good vinegar of your choice
    (balsamic or even raspberry)
2 tsp (1 dessertspoon) apple syrup
    (or maple syrup is an alternative)

A bunch of lightly chopped lettuce leaves
2–3 tbsp olive oil
3 tbsp hazelnuts
Sea salt
Sugar

In a food mixer beat the goat cheese and crème fraîche together with a pinch of good sea salt.

Peel the beets with a knife (it might be a little difficult), and then grate them. Mix the vinegar and a pinch each of salt and sugar. Set aside 1 to 2 tablespoons for the lettuce. Mix in the beets and let sit for 10 minutes to marinate.

Dress the chopped lettuce leaves with 2 to 3 tablespoons of olive oil and a tablespoon of the marinade from the beets.

You could pipe this on a plate with a pastry bag, but it is a rustic dish so big dollops work just as well.

Place the dressed lettuce leaves on a plate with the beet slaw. Add the goat cheese and drizzle with the syrup. Garnish with a few hazelnuts.

Serves 6

St. Tola Irish Goat Cheese

St. Tola Creamery, near Co. Clare's wild Atlantic coast, one of the premium artisan producers in Ireland, has been in operation since the early 1980s, with 200 milking goats on a 65-acre farm providing the milk for all the handmade cheese. The goats graze in fields with wild herbs and flowers, the tastes of which are part of the flavorful cheese. No additives or preservatives are used in producing the cheese. St. Tola Creamery takes pride in the fully traceable progression from farm to fork. The St. Tola log cheese was awarded the Euro-Toques Product of the Year Award–2015.

ABOVE: The goats are milked in groups while they munch on fresh feed.

BELOW: From start to finish; the progression from whey to award-winning St. Tola log cheese.

OPPOSITE: The goats graze in fields with flowers and wild herbs.

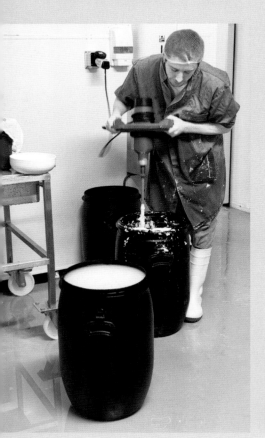

Sea Scallops with Puréed and Pickled Cauliflower

1 cauliflower
1 cup/240 ml whiskey
1 cup/240 ml vinegar
1 pinch salt
1 pinch sugar
½ cup/120 ml cream
1 cup/200 g butter + extra for cooking scallops
1 cup/240 ml water
1 cup/240 ml milk

24 large local scallops, 4 per person (roe removed and
    membrane peeled off)
Canola oil for cooking scallops
Salt and pepper to taste

NOTE: Our scallops are from Cleggan, a small picturesque fishing village in Connemara on the edge of the sea.

Make a pickling liquor with the whiskey, vinegar, salt, and sugar in a bowl.

Chop the cauliflower in half and thinly slice 1 half into the pickling liquor.

Heat the cream and butter together in a pan and keep warm.

Chop roughly and simmer the second half of the cauliflower in a pan with equal parts water and milk. When very soft, drain and purée in a blender, adding the hot cream and butter. Season to taste.

Pan fry the scallops several at a time in a hot heavy-bottom pan in a medium oil (canola), then add a little butter and baste. Don't crowd the scallops or move them around too much in the pan. Sear well to a good browned color. Season with salt and pepper to taste.

To serve, place some puréed cauliflower in the center of a plate, add the sautéed scallops on top with the pickled cauliflower pieces.

Serves 6

Lamb, Samphire, and Burnt Onion Purée

2¼ lb/1 kg organic white onions
7 fl oz/200 ml chicken stock
1¼ lb/500 g fresh samphire (broccoli can be substituted)
2½ lb /1.1 kg lamb loin fillet, 7 oz/200 g per person
Salt
Butter and oil for cooking

NOTE: Samphire is a bright green salty sea vegetable that grows on shorelines and marshes. Long green strands of samphire are in the photograph.

Cut the onions in half. Scoop out the middle with yout fingers to create a shell. Put the scooped out centers aside to save for another dish. Place the cut onions cut face down in a heavy-bottom frying pan and sear with a little oil until they are charred. Then lower the heat and cook until soft and the sweetness of the onion comes out. Set aside 1 or 2 of the onions to slice and use as a garnish on the serving plate. Using a blender, purée the rest of the onions in warm chicken stock.

NOTE: Use 2¼ lb/1 kg of broccoli If you substitute it for the samphire.

Blanch the samphire or the broccoli in slightly salty water. (As a sea herb, the samphire already has a saltiness of its own, so be careful not to oversalt.) Set aside.

Season the lamb and sear in a natural oil (canola) to a nice even color. Then add enough butter to the pan to baste heavily, allowing the foaming butter to cover the lamb. Remove the pan from the heat and let the lamb rest in the pan for 8 minutes to allow it to bake. Then heat to slowly cook through to a medium center.

Slice the charred onions set aside earlier.

Lightly warm the samphire or broccoli in butter.

Slice the lamb and serve with the lightly warmed samphire or broccoli and a good dollop of the onion puree. Garnish with a few sliced charred onions.

Serves 6

Rose Water Crème Brûlée

12–14 large egg yolks (approximately 225 ml)
1 cup/225 g superfine sugar
6¼ cups/1.5 L cream
2 tbsp rose water

Preheat oven to 325°F/160°C/Gas Mark 3.

Beat the egg yolks and sugar together in a bowl and set aside.

Add the cream to a pan and gently heat it on the stove. Then stir a small amount of the hot cream into the yolk and sugar mixture. When smooth, mix all the elements together including the rose water.

Pour into 6 ramekins and place in a pan with hot water about halfway up the sides of the ramekins and bake in the preheated oven for about 35 minutes.

Caramelize the top with a culinary torch.

Serves 6

NOTE: You can substitute any flavored syrup of your choice for the rose water. Eggnog and gingerbread syrups are favorites of mine at Christmas.

A long view of the river, woodlands, and mountains in the magical Connemara setting of Ballynahinch Castle.

Wood Pigeon, Gooseberry, and Spinach

1 lb/500 g gooseberries
½ cup/100 g sugar
1¼ cups/300 ml water
2 crowns of wood pigeon per person
1 cup/200 g soft butter
1½ lb/680 g raw baby leaf spinach
7 fl oz/200 ml sherry

Salt and pepper to season

Simmer the gooseberries and sugar in the water until soft—like jam. Set aside.

Season the wood pigeon with salt and pepper and rub generously with soft butter. Sear the wood pigeon on all sides in a hot, heavy-bottom frying pan, then baste all over with the butter. Rest in the pan for 8 minutes allowing the heat to gently cook the bird. Remove the wood pigeon from the pan and place on a plate.

In the same pan gently wilt the spinach and add the sherry.

To serve, place slices of the bird on a plate, add a serving of spinach and a dollop of the gooseberry compote.

Serves 4

NOTE: Squab is an alternate choice for the wood pigeon.

NOTE: If gooseberries are unavailable, nice ripe plums are suitable.

NOTE: I love the balance of cooking at the restaurant and cooking at home. When I cook at home it is more casual—in the preparation and the style. In the process I use every spoon, pot, utensil, and surface in the kitchen, and really enjoy it. I love informal dinner parties, casual and fun—a wonderful way for me to relax.

Sweaty Betty with Barley and Seaweed

NOTE: Sweaty Betty is a fish from the North Atlantic off the coast of Connemara. Cod is a fine alternate fish.

4 oz/110 g Sweaty Betty fillet per person
2¾ cups/500 g pearl barley
7 oz/200 g dried seaweed (available at all good health food stores)
Butter for cooking

Pre-soak the barley and seaweed for a few minutes in separate bowls of cold water to cover.

Remove the seaweed from the water and chop into small pieces.

Put the barley in a small pan with twice the amount of water (4½ cups of water to 2¼ cups of barley). Bring to a gentle simmer. When the barley softens, mix it with a big spoon of butter and the chopped up seaweed.

In a hot, wide-bottom frying pan sear the fish and cook on each side for 3 to 4 minutes to a nice golden crust. Then baste the fish with butter and let rest for 2 minutes.

Place a good dollop of barley in a bowl, top with the fish and spoon over the juices from the pan.

Serves 6

Foraging for seaweed at the ocean's edge.

Sheep Yogurt Mousse with Marinated Strawberries and Mint

3½ leaves gold gelatin or 1¾ tsp gelatin powder
½ cup/110 g superfine sugar
4 egg yolks
3½ cups/800 ml semi-whipped cream
½ cup/120 ml cream
2 vanilla beans
Generous 1 cup/250 g sheep yogurt
1 cup/200 g strawberries, sliced
10 mint leaves
2 tsp (1 dessertspoon) apple-cider vinegar
    (you can change this to your preference)

Soak the 3½ sheets of gelatin in a bowl of 3 cups of cold water for 5 to 10 minutes. When soft, squeeze the sheets to drain out the excess liquid before adding them to the liquid recipe ingredients. Or, if using gelatin powder, sprinkle it evenly over about ½ cup of cold water and let it set for a few minutes to "bloom."

Beat together the sugar and egg yolk.

Whip the 3½ cups of semi-whipped cream to very soft peaks.

Put the ½ cup of cream in a small pot and heat to a simmer. Add the vanilla beans and egg and sugar mixture. Cook gently for a few minutes, stirring constantly, until it thickens. Stir in the softened gelatin until it dissolves. Stir in the yogurt, and finally fold in the cream whipped to soft peaks.

Put into individual ramekins and put in the refrigerator to set for an hour or more.

Mix together in a bowl the sliced strawberries, mint leaves, and vinegar.

To serve, unmold the mousse onto a dessert plate and decorate with the strawberries and mint mixture.

Serves 6

Look closely. Are these sheep wearing sweaters?

Connemara Smokehouse

Owned and run by the Roberts family since 1979, Connemara Smokehouse on the edge of the Atlantic in Co. Galway is the oldest smokehouse in Connemara and the recipient of many awards. They are one of the few smokehouses specializing in smoking wild Atlantic

salmon adhering to time-honored traditional smoking methods using only the finest fresh fish, sourced locally, and natural ingredients. The fillets are sprinkled with a dry sea salt, which is left on for 8 to 10 hours depending on the size of the fish, and then washed off with fresh water and put inro a cold room for the water to run off. Then the fillets are placed in an oven with a slow-burning wood fire.

ABOVE CENTER: Pulling the dry-salted and washed salmon fillets from a slow-burning fire of aromaic wood shavings where they have been smoking for 8 to 10 hours.

ABOVE: Slicing the smoked salmon.

OPPOSITE: The Aillebrack Pier on the edge of the Atlantic, just next to the Connemara Smokehouse.

LEFT: John Roberts with a triumphant smile and a celebratory string of smoked salmon slices.

Renvyle House
Connemara
Co. Galway
Chef: Tim O'Sullivan

ABOVE: The Conservatory exterior of Renvyle House with a threatening sky.

Head Chef at Renvyle House restaurant in Connemara for over twenty years, Tim O'Sullivan has been a Commissioner of Euro-Toques Ireland and a participant in the New Irish Cuisine movement. Renvyle House is a historic four-star country house hotel situated on 150 acres in the beautiful, rugged, unspoiled landscape of Connemara on the shores of Ireland's Wild Atlantic Way. Once the home of Oliver St. John Gogarty (Buck Mulligan of James Joyce's "Ulysses.") W. B. Yeats spent his honeymoon here.

MENUS

LUNCH

**Scallops on a Pea Purée with Vegetable Butter Sauce
and Crispy Pancetta**

**Homemade Pork and Apple Sausage with
Shallot and Sage Mashed Potatoes and Port Jus**

TEA

Chocolate Steamed Pudding

DINNER ONE

Mussel Pie with Chive Mashed Potatoes

**Atlantic Way Duet: Rack of Lamb and
Atlantic Lobster with Spinach and Tomato Fondue**

Renvyle House Berry Trifle

DINNER TWO

West Coast Seafood Chowder

Crispy Breast of Duckling with Root Vegetables

Rhubarb and Ginger Crème Brûlée

ABOVE: Tim O'Sullivan, Head Chef at Renvyle House.

LEFT: The main dining room at Renvyle House.

Scallops on a Pea Purée with Vegetable Butter Sauce and Crispy Pancetta

½ cup/120 ml water
2⅔ cups/400 g peas
7 fl oz/200 ml cream
14 tbsp butter
12 scallops, shelled and cleaned
Salt and black pepper
Juice of ¼ lemon
½ cup/100 g vegetables, combination of shallots, celery,
    carrots, and fennel
½ cup/120 ml white-wine vinegar
4 slices pancetta (Italian bacon)
Olive oil
Fennel sprigs, for garnish

Preheat oven to 425°F/220°C/Gas Mark 7.

Bring the water to a boil in a saucepan. Add the peas and cook for 6 minutes. Strain and purée in a blender with a little cream and about 4 tablespoons butter.

Season the scallops with salt, pepper, and lemon juice.

Place the vegetables and white-wine vinegar in a saucepan and cook over medium heat for 3 to 4 minutes. Add the cream and cook until reduced by a third. Remove from the heat, whisk in 10 tablespoons of butter. Keep warm.

Place the pancetta on a baking sheet and cook in the preheated oven for 10 minutes. Reheat the pea purée.

Heat a light coating of oil in a hot pan; add the scallops and cook for 2 to 3 minutes on each side. Place on paper towels and keep warm.

Spoon some pea purée on warmed plates. Place scallops on top. Dress with the sauce and pancetta. Garnish with fennel sprigs.

Serves 4

Homemade Pork and Apple Sausage with Shallot and Sage Mashed Potatoes and Port Jus

4 potatoes
2½ fl oz/70 ml cream
2 tbsp butter, softened
Salt and pepper
2 shallots
3–4 sage leaves
3½ fl oz/100 ml port
1 orange for zests
1 tsp grated ginger
2 tbsp red currant jelly
Generous ½ cup/125 g red currants
1 tsp finely chopped thyme
4 homemade pork and apple sausages
Olive oil for cooking
4 sprigs parsley

NOTE: We make this dish with fresh homemade sausages from Kelly's Artisan Butchers in Co. Mayo. You should search for the best local homemade sausages near you.

Wash, peel, and cut the potatoes into 4 to 6 pieces. Place in a pan with water to cover; boil on medium heat for 25 minutes.

Meanwhile bring the cream to a boil in a saucepan. Strain and purée the potatoes, adding the soft butter and boiling cream and mix until smooth.

Finely dice the shallots and finely chop the sage. Sauté the shallots without browning in olive oil and add the sage; cook gently for another minute. Mix the shallot-sage mixture into the potato purée. Keep warm until served.

Boil the port, then add the orange zest, grated ginger, thyme, and red currant jelly until it is reduced by one third. Add the red currants and boil for 3 minutes. Strain through a sieve and keep warm until served.

Cook the sausages in a hot frying pan. Cut them into several pieces each. Pipe the hot potato-sage purée on a warm serving plate, place the cut sausage on top of the purée and drizzle the port jus on top of that. Garnish with some parsley leaves.

Serves 4

Chocolate Steamed Pudding

Homemade chocolate from Wilde Irish Handmade Artisan Chocolate.

NOTE: For the photograph we added some vanilla ice cream and embellished the plate with a design of piped caramelized sugar with fruit purée.

FOR THE FILLING
3 fl oz/80 ml cream
4 oz/100 g good chocolate
2 tsp brandy

FOR THE PUDDING CAKE
8 tbsp butter, softened
½ cup/100 g superfine sugar
2 medium eggs
¾ cup/90 g cake flour
½ cup/50 g cocoa powder
Confectioners' sugar for dusting

Preheat oven to 400°F/200°C/Gas Mark 6.

To make the filling, heat the cream in a saucepan until hot but not boiling. Remove from the heat and add the chocolate. Stir until melted and add the brandy. Pour into a bowl and chill for 2 to 3 hours.

To make the pudding cake, lightly grease four 5-oz/150-ml ramekins. Line the bases with parchment paper.

Cream together the butter and sugar in a bowl. Gradually add the eggs, beating well. Sift the flour and cocoa powder into the mixture and stir lightly.

Spoon 1 tablespoon of the pudding mixture into each ramekin. Add a ball of chocolate filling on top. Top this with another layer of the pudding mixture. Level and cover with parchment paper. Secure with string.

Place the ramekins on a grill rack over a roasting pan half-filled with boiling water. Cover with foil, place in the oven, and cook for 30 to 35 minutes.

Turn the puddings out onto warmed serving plates and dust with confectioners' sugar.

Serves 4

Mussel Pie with Chive Mashed Potatoes

MUSSEL FILLING
30 mussels, washed and de-bearded
¼ cup/50 ml white wine
1 tbsp fresh dill, chopped
1 tbsp butter
2 tbsp carrot, diced
2 tbsp fennel, diced
2 shallots, diced
3 tsp flour
2 tbsp mussel stock
3 tbsp cream
Salt and pepper

Place the mussels in a pot with dill and white wine. Cook for 3 to 4 minutes. Take the mussels out of the pot (reserve the mussel stock) and remove the mussels from their shells. Discard any mussels that did not open. Place in a bowl and keep warm.

Heat a pan and add the butter and then the carrot, fennel, and shallots. Cook for 2 to 3 minutes. Add the flour to thicken the mix. Add the reserved white wine and mussel stock, cook for 2 minutes, then add the cream and dill, followed by the mussels.

CHIVE MASHED POTATOES
4–6 potatoes, peeled and quartered
4 tbsp butter
3½ fl oz/100 ml cream
4 tbsp chives, chopped

Put the potatoes in a pot of salted water and bring to a boil. Cook for 25 minutes. Drain, mash, and transfer to a bowl. Heat the cream for 2 to 3 minutes, add butter and chives, and allow butter to melt. Add the potatoes and mix. Season to taste. Keep warm.

To serve, line a pie bowl with some of the chive mashed potatoes, fill with the mussel mix. Top with more mashed potatoes.

Serves 4

Atlantic Way Duet:
Rack of Lamb and Atlantic Lobster with Spinach and Tomato Fondue

NOTE: An oven-ready rack of lamb (Frenched) has had the fat, meat, and cartilage removed from between the bones. This offers an elegant presentation.

NOTE: If you use fresh bread-crumbs, you would need 4 cups.

2 Frenched racks of lamb (1 kg)
Salt, black pepper
Olive oil for searing
1 tsp Dijon mustard
1¾ cups/200 g dried bread crumbs
1 tsp chopped mixed herbs
  (parsley, thyme, mint)
4 tsp (2 dessertspoons) chopped rosemary

2 lobsters (2 kg)

RED WINE JUS
¼ cup/50 ml red wine
3½ fl oz/100 ml lamb stock
1 tbsp red currant jelly
1 tbsp cilantro, chopped
Salt, black pepper

Bring 5¼ quarts/5 liters of salted water to boil for the lobsters.

Heat the oven to 400°F/200°C/Gas Mark 6.

Season the lamb with salt and pepper. Heat a little olive oil in a large sauté pan and sear the lamb on both sides; add a little rosemary, and place in a roasting pan in the preheated oven for 12 minutes or more, until cooked as you like it.

To finish the lamb, coat the outside surface with a mixture of the mustard, crumbs, and herbs. Finish under a hot grill for 2 minutes to crisp and brown. Keep warm.

Place the lobsters in the pot of boiling water and simmer for 10 to 12 minutes. Remove from the water, set aside, and keep warm.

When ready to serve, split the lobsters in half and remove the heads, leaving the meat in the tails. Remove the meat from the claws by crushing the shells.

For the red wine jus, mix the red wine, lamb stock, currant jelly, cilantro leaves, and salt and pepper in a pot and simmer over low heat for 3 to 4 minutes. Pour into a serving cup or ramekin.

SPINACH AND TOMATO FONDUE

Olive oil for sautéeing
2 shallots, diced
2 cloves garlic, chopped
1 lb/450 g spinach

¼ cup/50 ml cream
2 fresh tomatoes, peeled and diced
10 tbsp butter
2 tbsp lemon juice

Heat a pan and add oil, shallots, and garlic. Cook for 2 to 3 minutes. Add spinach, cream, tomato, butter, and lemon juice. Simmer for 2 minutes.

Serves 4

NOTE: The basic dish— the lamb, lobster, and spinach-tomato fondue— is what I would prepare at home. When presenting this at the restaurant we dress it up with extra sides and garnish.

Renvyle House Berry Trifle

3½ fl oz/100 ml cream
1½ cup/120 g berries (raspberries, strawberries,
    and blueberries) at room temperature
¼ cup/50 g sugar
1 cup/200 g mascarpone cheese
⅔ cup/130 g cream cheese
1 egg
2 tbsp lemon liqueur
6 amaretti biscuits (crushed)
1 tbsp flaked almonds (toasted)

Whip the cream to soft peaks. Set aside.

Mix the berries in a bowl with 1 tablespoon of sugar. Set aside to allow juices to be released from the berries. Stir occasionally.

In a separate bowl, stir the mascarpone and cream cheese to soften.

Then whisk together the egg and remaining sugar, add the whipped cream, and the mascarpone and cream cheese mixture.

Layer 4 glasses with crushed amaretti biscuits, saving a bit for the top. Then add a layer of the cheese and whipped cream mixture, followed by a layer of berries. Save a few berries to place on the top.

Add the lemon liqueur to the remaining cheese and whipped cream mixture. Spoon a generous dollop of this on top of the berries in the dessert dish—glass or ramekin. Top with almonds and more crushed amaretti biscuits. Garnish with a few berries.

Chill for 2 to 3 hours.

Serves 4

NOTE: Amaretti biscuits are a traditional Italian almond-flavored macaroon, crispy on the outside and chewy on the inside.

West Coast Seafood Chowder

¼ cup/50 g butter
¾ cup/150 g combined diced carrots, leeks, and celery
2 onions, diced
3 medium potatoes, cooked, cubed
2 bay leaves
2 tbsp brandy
6 cups/1½ liter fish stock
1 cup/240 ml milk
¾ lb/340 g cubed fish: smoked haddock, cod, shrimp,
    mussels, salmon, and monkfish
Salt and pepper
Generous ½ cup/125 ml cream
4 tbsp chopped parsley

Melt the butter in a large pot; add carrots, leeks, celery, and onion and sauté for 3 to 4 minutes.

Add potatoes, bay leaves, and brandy and cook for a further 3 minutes. Add fish stock and milk and bring to a boil. Then add the fish and simmer for 5 to 8 minutes over a medium heat.

Add cream and parsley, season with salt and pepper, and bring back to a boil.

Ladle the chowder into warm soup plates. Serve with homemade brown bread.

Serves 4 to 6

A fisherman repairs his net on a pier.

Crispy Breast of Duckling with Root Vegetables

4 tbsp each of the following vegetables:
  Parsnips
  Carrots
  Bok choy
  Celeriac
  Baby leeks
Salt and pepper
1 cup/240 ml olive oil
1 tsp grated ginger

4 duck breasts

Generous ¾ cup/170 g green cabbage

¼ cup/60 ml cream
2 oz/50 g butter
4 tbsp sweet chili sauce, more for garnish
1 egg white
4 slices eggplant
2 tbsp sesame seeds
Fresh herbs, for garnish

Preheat the oven to 350°F/180°C/Gas Mark 4.

Peel and cube the vegetables. Steam them for 10 minutes, and then sauté in a pan with a little oil and ginger for 10 minutes. Remove from the heat, season to taste, and keep warm.

Season the duck breasts. In a hot pan heat some oil and sear the duck breasts on both sides. Then place in the preheated oven for 10 to 15 minutes. When cooked, place in a baking pan under the broiler for a few minutes to crisp the skin.

Shred the cabbage very fine and deep fry in hot oil until crispy. Drain on paper towels.

Put the cream and butter in a saucepan, bring to a simmer, and reduce by half. Then mix in the sweet chili sauce.

Stir the egg white in a soup plate. Season the eggplant slices and dip into the egg white and then coat with sesame seeds. Heat some oil in a frying pan, add the eggplant and fry until crispy.

To serve, stack the cubed vegetables in the center of warm plates and place the eggplant on top. Layer the duck on the eggplant and the cabbage on top of that. Spoon some sauce on the plate and garnish with the diced vegetables, some fresh herbs, and a few dabs of sweet chili sauce.

Serves 4

Rhubarb and Ginger Crème Brûlée

1¼ cups/300 ml cream
⅔ cup/150 ml milk
1 vanilla bean (or 2–2½ tsp vanilla extract)
8 egg yolks
½ cup/100 g superfine sugar
½ cup/50 g diced and cooked rhubarb
1 tsp grated ginger
½ cup/100 g brown sugar
4 sprigs of mint, for garnish

Preheat the oven to 350°F/180°C/Gas Mark 4.

Put cream, milk, and vanilla in a saucepan and bring to a gentle simmer over medium heat.

Whisk the egg yolks and the superfine sugar together in a large bowl.

When the cream/milk mixture is hot, pour through a sieve onto the egg yolk and sugar mixture and stir well. Then add the rhubarb and mix in the grated ginger.

Divide the mixture into 4 ramekins. Fill a shallow roasting pan with water half way up the sides. Place the ramekins in the pan and bake in the preheated oven for approximately 45 minutes. Remove the dishes from the water and place in the refrigerator to chill for 2 to 3 hours.

To serve, take the rhubarb and ginger crème brûlée out of the refrigerator approximately 30 minutes before serving. Sprinkle the brown sugar evenly over the top of the brûlée and caramelize with a culinary torch, or put under the broiler for a few seconds. Garnish with a fresh mint leaf and serve.

Serves 4

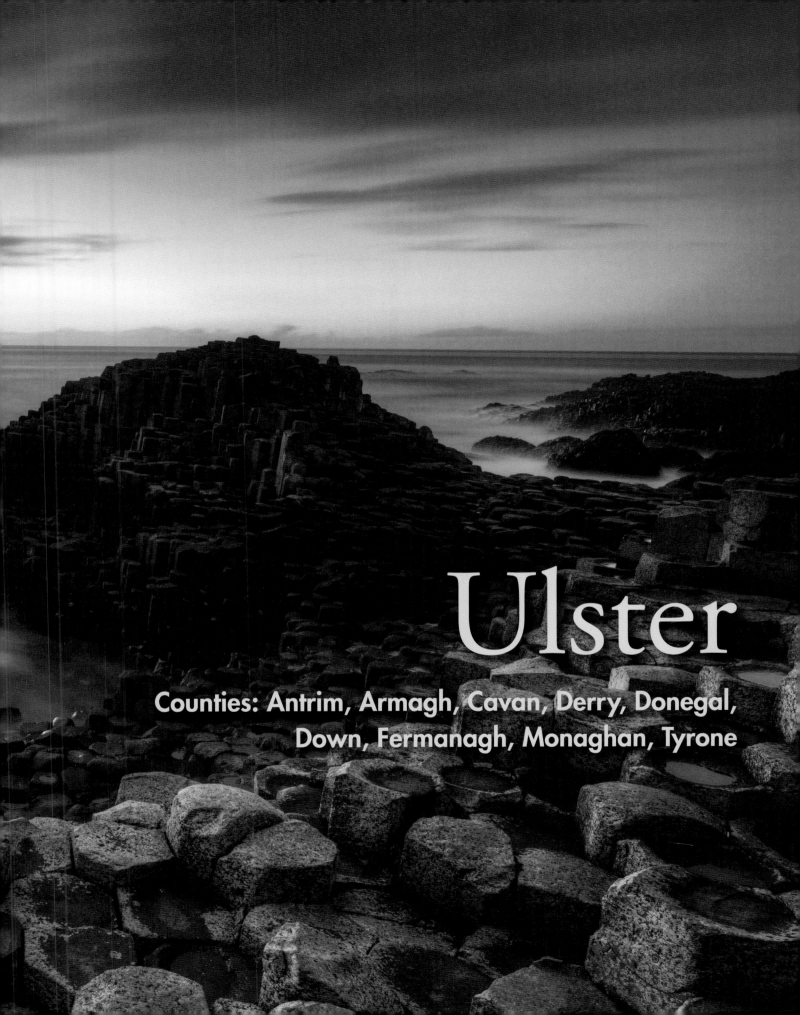

Ulster

Counties: Antrim, Armagh, Cavan, Derry, Donegal, Down, Fermanagh, Monaghan, Tyrone

PREVIOUS SPREAD: The Giant's Causeway in Co. Antrim is an extraordinary geological formation. History tells us that this collection of tubular basalt structures is the result of volcanic action millions of years ago, but according to legend the giant Finn McCool built the promontory as a pathway across the sea to Scotland.

RIGHT: Master butchers are a pride of country towns across the region.

OPPOSITE TOP: The peaceful landscape with the Mourne Mountains in Co. Down inspired the setting of C.S Lewis's *The Chronicles of Narnia* and the fascinating world of *Game of Thrones*.

OPPOSITE BOTTOM: The wild Atlantic Ocean on the coast of Donegal is a mesmerizing presence.

The province of Ulster encompasses nine counties—Antrim, Armagh, Cavan, Derry, Donegal, Down, Fermanagh, Monaghan and Tyrone – of which Cavan, Donegal and Monaghan are part of the Irish Republic. The remaining six form Northern Ireland, part of the United Kingdom of Great Britain and Ireland, with a majority Protestant population. The western part of the province was the last part of the country conquered by the English around 1600, and was thereafter partially planted by settlers and other arrivals from Britain, who have brought a distinctive accent, dialect, and customs to the province.

Northern Ireland's scenery is enhanced by a number of mountains, including Errigal in Donegal, the Sperrins in Tyrone (possibly a source of some of Ireland's glistening prehistoric gold), the mountains of Antrim with their Glens facing Scotland with which they had close ties, and also the Mourne Mountains in County Down which famously 'sweep down to the sea' in Percy French's lyric ballad. Its three main rivers flow through important towns, the Foyle through Derry, the Bann through Coleraine and the Lagan through Belfast, once a mighty boat-building center which launched the Titanic. The province proudly contains Ireland's largest lake, Lough Neagh, well-known for its eels. Killybegs in Donegal prides itself on a large

RIGHT: Belfast has grown from a small market town to a thriving metropolis. The Titanic was built in its famous Harland and Wolff shipyard.

RIGHT: A traffic jam on the country roads of Northern Ireland can frequently mean something other than cars! Drivers and sheep adjust.

OPPOSITE TOP: Spectacularly sited Dunluce Castle sits on a narrow basalt outcrop stretching into the Atlantic on the north coast of Co. Antrim. In the 17th century the extreme right section of the structure collapsed into the sea bringing some of the staff with it.

OPPOSITE BOTTOM: The popular Duke of York bar tucked in a narrow alley in Belfast.

sea-fishing fleet. Ulster is a province rich in cattle, sheep, pigs and poultry which provide the province and beyond with protein, while oats and barley are the grains most cultivated. Potatoes are much prized along the northern coastal counties, and Armagh is one of the finest apple-growing areas in the whole island of Ireland. The orchards are to be found among the drumlins—humps left by the retreating glaciers twenty thousand years ago, creating a charming network of curving roads to drive between them.

—**Peter Harbison**

Browns Restaurant
Derry
Co. Derry
Northern Ireland
Chef: Ian Orr

BELOW: Browns restaurant in Derry/Londonderry, named Best Restaurant in Ulster in 2013 and again in 2016, and Best Restaurant in Northern Ireland 2013.

OPPOSITE, BOTTOM: Ardtara Castle, site of Ian Orr's newest award-winning restaurant.

Since opening Browns Restaurant in 2009, Ian Orr has opened two more Browns in Derry and another Browns at Ardtara Castle near the village of Upperlands in Co. Londonderry. One of Ireland's top multi-award winning talents, Ian was named Chef of the Year in 2013. In 2015 Browns became the only restaurant in Northern Ireland to be invited into the prestigious "Ireland's Blue Book." He is known for his light touch allowing the natural flavor, texture, and color of fresh ingredients to take center stage.

MENUS

LUNCH

Goat Cheese, Endive, and Walnut Salad

Pork Fillet with Roasted Butternut Squash, Mushrooms, Lemon, and Parsley

DINNER ONE

Seared Scallops with Black Pudding Crumb and Homemade Potato Bread

Beef Fillet with Buttered Spinach, Dulse Seaweed Hollandaise

Chocolate Fondant

DINNER TWO

Gin-Cured Salmon and Pickled Cucumber with Dill

Lamb with Spinach, Goat Curd Cheese, and Toasted Pine Nuts

Vanilla Panna Cotta with Honeycomb

ABOVE: The *Bridgestone Guide* has said of Ian Orr (above) that he will be one of the most celebrated of a new generation of chefs in Ireland.

Goat Cheese, Endive, and Walnut Salad

2 heads endive
2 tbsp crème fraîche
2 tbsp lemon Juice
1 bunch mint, chopped
7 oz/200 g mixed salad leaves
3 tbsp extra virgin olive oil
4 tbsp/60 g toasted walnuts
4 tbsp/60 g goat cheese

Slice the endive into long pieces. In a small bowl mix the crème fraîche with the lemon juice and chopped mint.

In a larger bowl toss together the mixed salad leaves and endive and finally add the olive oil. Place on a plate and add the chopped nuts and goat cheese.

Serves 4

Fivemiletown Creamery, award-winning artisan cheesemakers in Co. Tyrone, is a farmer-owned cooperative producing specialty cheeses. We have used Fivemiletown Creamery's handmade soft, creamy Boilie pearls goat cheese in this salad.

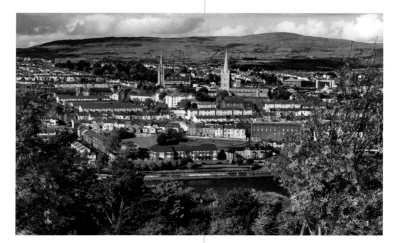

A long view of the town of Derry from across the river.

Pork Fillet with Roasted Butternut Squash, Mushrooms, Lemon, and Parsley

NOTE: As an interesting variation, purée some of the squash to use as a garnish. Add a light sauce made from the meat drippings and broth.

NOTE: A sautéed, grilled slice of oyster mushroom is the garnish at the center of the plate in the photograph.

1 butternut squash, peeled and cut into small cubes
1–2 tbsp olive oil, as needed for cooking
8 chestnut mushrooms, cut into quarters
1 tbsp butter
1 tsp honey
Juice of 1 lemon
1 bunch parsley, chopped
1 pork fillet, trimmed

Preheat the oven to 350°F/180°C/Gas Mark 4.

Place the squash in boiling salted water for 5 minutes, and then strain and cool.

In a large skillet add a little oil and sauté the squash on a medium heat for about 4 minutes. Add the mushrooms and cook for 2 minutes more. Then add butter, honey, lemon, and parsley, and season to taste.

In another pan, season the pork and cook in a little oil for 3 minutes on each side. Then place into the preheated oven and cook for 5 minutes. Remove from the oven to rest for several minutes before slicing.

Place the butternut squash mix on a plate and add the sliced pork.

Serves 4

Seared Scallops with Black Pudding Crumb and Homemade Potato Bread

FOR THE POTATO BREAD
4 medium potatoes, peeled and halved
⅔ cup/75 g plain flour
Salt and pepper, to taste
Oil, for frying

FOR THE SCALLOPS
8 slices of local black pudding
1 tbsp butter
12 scallops
2 tbsp olive oil
1 lemon
Fresh parsley, for garnish (optional)

Preheat the oven to 350°F/180°C/Gas Mark 4.

To make the potato bread, boil the potatoes in salted water at a medium heat for about 20 minutes until easily pierced with a fork. Drain the potatoes and let them dry. Place the cooked, dry potatoes into a bowl and mash them with the flour. Season with salt and pepper and mix until the dough is firm. Knead the dough on a well-floured surface and roll flat into a 9-inch circle. Cut the dough like a pie into 4 pieces. Cook the slices—farls—on a lightly oiled skillet or frying pan for 3 minutes on each side.

Place the black pudding and butter onto a baking pan and crumble with your hands. Bake for 15 minutes in the preheated oven until nice and crumbly.

Now season the scallops with salt and freshly ground pepper and rub with oil. Cook in a hot skillet for 1 minute each side. Finish with a squeeze of lemon.

Place the potato bread onto plates, top with scallops, and sprinkle with black pudding crumble. Garnish with fresh parsley or another light herb if you wish.

Serves 4

NOTE: Black pudding in Ireland is a blood sausage mixed with oatmeal—a mainstay of a full Irish breakfast and the Ulster fry. And now it is no longer served only at breakfast. If the black sausage is not available to you or, if you prefer, you could garnish with toasted or carmelized crumbled pecans, or 1 or 2 strips of cooked and crumbled bacon.

NOTE: We used scallops from Greencastle Harbor in Co. Donegal.

Beef Fillet with Buttered Spinach, Dulse Seaweed Hollandaise

FOR THE DULSE HOLLANDAISE
Generous 2 cups/500 ml white-wine vinegar
1 tbsp peppercorn
3 large egg yolks
2 tbsp dulse seaweed, rehydrated in hot water and
    then chopped roughly
2 tbsp butter
Squeeze of lemon

FOR THE BEEF
2 lb/900 g beef fillet, or 4 fillets, each about 8 oz/225 g
1½ lb/680 g baby spinach
2 tbsp butter
Oil for searing
Salt and pepper to taste

Preheat the oven to 350°F/180°C/Gas Mark 4.

For the hollandaise, boil the vinegar together with the peppercorns until reduced by half, strain and reserve.

Place a bowl on top of but not touching simmering water. Add the egg yolks and 2 tbsp of the vinegar mix to the bowl, and start to whisk. Whisk and add more vinegar until the mixture doubles in size, then take off the heat and slowly add the butter to make a smooth sauce. Add a squeeze of lemon and the dulse, and mix.

Now sear the beef for 1 to 2 minutes on each side in a hot oven-proof pan with a little seasoning and oil, and place in the preheated oven for 6 to 8 minutes for the 2 lb fillet for medium (shorter or longer to cook to your preference). Turn the meat over and cook for another 1 to 2 minutes. Remove the beef from the pan and set aside to rest.

In the same pan add the butter and cook the spinach for 1 to 2 minutes, then serve with the sliced fillet or fillets.

Put the spinach on a plate and add the beef. Collect the roasting juices in a sauceboat and place on the table.

Serves 4

NOTE: If you prefer, use any steak of your choice.

NOTE: Dried seaweed is available at most health food stores.

NOTE: If preparing the individual fillets, sear them for about 2 minutes on each side.

NOTE: Spinach shrinks in cooking to about one-tenth of its original weight.

Chocolate Fondant

½ cup/100 g butter
About 4 oz/100 g good dark chocolate
½ cup/120 g superfine sugar
2 whole eggs + 2 egg yolks
Scant 1 cup/100 g plain flour

Preheat the oven to 350°F/180°C.

Butter 6 ramekins and set aside.

Melt the butter and chocolate together in a bowl set over a pan of lightly simmering water.

Beat the sugar and eggs together in a second bowl and then add that to the chocolate and butter mix.

Fold in the flour and mix together well.

Pour the mixture into the 6 buttered ramekins.

Just before serving place the 6 ramekins on a baking sheet and place in the preheated oven for 10 minutes. When done, release each warm cake from the ramekin and quickly place on a plate. Serve immediately with some whipped cream or ice cream.

Serves 6

Dark chocolate from Wilde Irish Chocolate.

Gin-Cured Salmon and Pickled Cucumber with Dill

FOR THE SALMON
2 tbsp salt
3½ tbsp sugar
1 lemon zest
1¼ lb/500 g salmon fillet, skinned
2 tbsp dill, chopped
3½ fl oz/100 ml Shortcross Gin®

FOR THE PICKLED CUCUMBER
3 tbsp white-wine vinegar
3½ fl oz/100 ml water
2 tbsp sugar
1 sprig thyme
1 cucumber, peeled and sliced

1 sprig of dill, for garnish

Place the salt, sugar, lemon zest, and chopped dill together and rub all over the salmon; pour the gin over it and place for 2 days in a covered bowl in the refrigerator to cure. At the end of 2 days, remove the salmon from the refrigerator and rinse under cold water, dry with a cloth, and return to the refrigerator.

To make the pickling liquid, warm the vinegar and water in a saucepan on the stove top. Add the sugar and thyme and keep on a low heat for a few minutes. Remove from the heat and set aside to cool.

When the pickling liquid is cool add the cucumber and set aside.

When ready to serve, cut the salmon into thin slices, add the cucumber, and finish with the dill. Serve with some bread or crackers.

Serves 4

Lamb with Spinach, Goat Curd Cheese, and Toasted Pine Nuts

4 lamb loins, 6 oz/150 g each
Approximately 2 tbsp oil
1½ lb/680 g spinach
Scant ½ cup/100 g goat curd cheese
2 tbsp pine nuts

Preheat oven to 350°F/180°C/Gas Mark 4.

Place the lamb in a hot skillet with a little oil on the stove top and sear for about 2 minutes. Then place the skillet with the lamb in the preheated oven for 5 minutes. Remove from the oven and place the lamb on a platter to rest for a few minutes.

In the same pan cook the spinach on the stove top in batches with a little olive oil. Put as much spinach as fits easily in the pan for each batch. Remove the spinach and add the pine nuts to the same pan with more oil if necessary. Use a minimum amount of oil, just enough to prevent the pine nuts from sticking to the pan. Just brown them slightly.

Place the spinach on a plate and add the lamb, toasted pine nuts, dollops of goat curd cheese, and roasting juices.

Serves 4

NOTE: Spinach shrinks in cooking to about one-tenth of its original weight.

A serene Ulster landscape.

Vanilla Panna Cotta with Honeycomb

FOR THE PANNA COTTA
1½ cups/350 ml cream
1 cup/240 ml milk
Generous ⅓ cup/80 g sugar
1 vanilla bean
2 gelatin leaves, soaked in cold water, or 1 tsp gelatin powder

FOR THE HONEYCOMB
½ cup/100 g sugar
2 tbsp corn syrup
2 tbsp honey
2 tbsp water
2 tsp baking soda

NOTE: Bloom the 2 gelatin leaves by soaking them in 2 cups of very cold water for 5 to 10 minutes, until softened. Remove the leaves (also referred to as "sheets") from the water and gently squeeze the excess liquid from them. Then add the softened leaves to the warm mixture.

Warm the cream, milk, sugar, and vanilla in a saucepan and add the bloomed gelatin leaves (see note in margin). Or, if using gelatin powder, sprinkle it evenly over about ¼ cup of cold water and let it sit for a few minutes to "bloom," and then add it to the warm mix in the saucepan. Remove from the heat. When cool, pour the mixture into ramekins and place in the refrigerator for about an hour to set.

To make honeycomb, heat the sugar, corn syrup, honey, and water in a saucepan on the stove top and cook until golden. Remove from the heat and add the baking soda. When it doubles in size pour into a baking pan and let it cool. When it is cool, break into pieces.

To serve, place a ramekin on a dessert plate and add some honeycomb pieces. Or, if you prefer, unmold the ramekins onto a dessert plate and add the honeycomb. Garnish with fresh berries or anything of your choice.

Serves 4

Lough Erne Resort
Enniskillen
Co. Fermanagh
Northern Ireland
Chef: Noel McMeel

RIGHT: The elegant dining room at Lough Erne Resort, with doors opened to the spectacular views of The Fermanagh Lakelands.

Noel McMeel, Executive Head Chef at Lough Erne Resort in Co. Enniskillen, has introduced his own particular brand of modern Irish cooking to a new and discerning audience. Noel McMeel arrived at Lough Erne Resort with a simple philosophy: sourcing, preparing, and serving fresh food in season. In Northern Ireland the chefs are fortunate to have available some of the finest ingredients, a diverse array of superb raw material. Noel's passion for food and his vibrant energy inspire not only his team of chefs but the best local suppliers as well.

MENUS

LUNCH

Traditional Fish and Chips

**Smoked Irish Salmon, Cream Cheese,
and Traditional Boxty**

DINNER ONE

**Roast Artichoke Soup with
Caramelized Armagh Apple and Hazelnut Brittle**

Lough Erne Pork Dish

Raspberry Cheesecake and Strawberry Lemonade

DINNER TWO

**Crab and Scallops with Seaweed-Avocado Purée
and Fresh Lemon Curd**

**Fillet of Beef Bourguignon with
Mushroom Duxcelles, Pearl Onions, and
Roast Beef Sauce**

ABOVE: Noel McMeel on the grounds of Lough Erne, holding a platter of his signature dish, sophisticated Lough Erne Pork.

LEFT: Noel McMeel (center) with two of his team working on the presentation of one of the dishes for our photo shoot—Crab and Scallops with Seaweed-Avocado Purée and Fresh Lemon Curd.

Traditional Fish and Chips

Oil, for frying, enough to fill the fryer by two-thirds

FOR THE CHIPS
8 large floury potatoes (Russet)

FOR THE FISH
4 cod fillets, each 7 oz/200 g
2 cups/220 g cake flour, plus extra for dusting
1 tbsp Irish sea salt and ground white pepper
11 fl oz/325 ml good beer

Preheat the fryer to 250°F/120°C. Add oil to the fryer.

For the chips, peel the potatoes and cut into whatever size you prefer. Wash well in cold water, drain, and pat dry with a clean tea towel or paper towels. Put the potatoes into the preheated fryer filled about two-thirds with oil and allow them to fry gently for about 8 to 10 minutes or more as necessary. Lift out of the pan with a slotted spoon, and place on paper towels.

Increase the heat of the fryer to 350°F/180°C.

Season the fish and dust lightly with flour; this enables the batter to stick to the fish.

To make the batter, sift the flour and a pinch of salt into a large bowl and whisk in the beer to give a thick batter, adding a little extra beer if it seems over-thick. It should be the consistency of very thick double cream and should coat the back of a wooden spoon. Season with salt. Thickly coat the fillets with the batter and carefully place in the hot fat and cook for 8 to 10 minutes until golden and crispy. Once the fish is cooked, remove and place on paper towels and return the chips to the fryer and cook for 2 to 3 minutes or until golden and crispy. Shake off any excess oil and season with salt before serving with the crispy fish.

Serve with tartar sauce and half a lemon wrapped in cheesecloth.

Serves 4

NOTE: We used Innishmacsaint Fermanagh beer. Choose a beer that you enjoy.

NOTE: I think it is most important that the fish and chips be fried in a deep fryer. The deep fryer offers more stability.

NOTE: At home I would prepare the fish and chips in the oven or pan fried on the stove top without any batter. I probably would use half the fish fillet per person and serve with salad.

Smoked Irish Salmon, Cream Cheese, and Traditional Boxty

FOR THE BOXTY

¾ cup/125 g raw peeled potato (a floury variety such as Russet)
¾ cup/125 g mashed potato, made from 7 oz/200 g floury potatoes, peeled, cooked and mashed
Scant 1¼ cup/125 g plain flour, plus extra for dusting
½ tsp baking powder
½ tsp salt
Large knob salted butter, melted and cooled
A little milk, if necessary
Oil, for frying

Juice of 1 lemon
¼ cup/50 g olive oil
Fresh herb salad greens

½ cup/100 g cream cheese
4 oz/110 g thinly sliced smoked salmon (4 slices)

To make the boxty pancakes, grate the raw potato into a bowl. Turn out onto a cloth and wring over a bowl, catching the liquid. This will separate into a clear fluid with starch at the bottom. Pour off and discard the fluid, then scrape out the starch and mix it with the grated and mashed potatoes.

Sift the flour, baking powder, and salt and mix into the potatoes with the melted butter, adding a little milk if necessary to make a pliable dough. Knead lightly on a floured surface. Cut into ¼ cup/50 g portions and flatten like a pancake. Heat the pan with some olive oil and panfry until light brown on each side.

Make a dressing for the salad greens with the olive oil and lemon juice.

Place the warm boxty in the center of a plate, add a spoon of cream cheese, and place the smoked salmon on top with some lightly dressed fresh herb salad greens.

Serves 4

Boxty is a traditional Irish potato pancake that contains a mixture of mashed and grated potatoes, resulting in a unique texture. While suitable on an Irish breakfast or supper table, boxty pairs well with many cuisines for a meal at any time of day.

NOTE: We like to use oak smoked salmon at Lough Erne.

NOTE: Our cream cheese is from Fivemiletown Creamery in Co. Tyrone.

Roast Artichoke Soup with Caramelized Armagh Apple and Hazelnut Brittle

NOTE: We use fresh artichokes in our restaurant, but canned artichokes are an alternative and easy to use. Frozen articokes are another option, but be sure to defrost and dry them with a paper towel before proceeding.

NOTE: If using canned artichokes, taste one of the artichokes before roasting to check on the salt level; add salt only if necessary.

28–30 canned artichoke hearts, drained
2 tbsp rapeseed or extra-virgin olive oil
Salt, black pepper
3½ cups/750 ml vegetable stock
6 cups/1.5 L water
9–10 shallots
1¼ cups/300 ml cream
1 clove garlic, peeled
Scant 1⅓ cups/200 g sliced potatoes

FOR THE CARAMELIZED APPLE
2 Granny Smith apples, peeled
1⅓ cups/300 g sugar
Juice of 1 lemon

Preheat the oven to 400°F/200°C/Gas Mark 6.

Place the canned artichoke hearts with a little oil, salt and pepper in a roasting pan in the preheated oven for 15 minutes. Canned artichokes are already cooked; but this step will provide a deeper flavor to them.

Put the vegetable stock and water into a saucepan and bring to a simmer. In another pan sweat off (cook with no color) the shallot and garlic at a low heat for a few minutes (essentially drying to release their juices). Add these to the stock along with the sliced potatoes and roasted artichoke hearts. Simmer for 10 to 15 minutes. Add the cream and cook for a further 2 minutes. Season to taste. Place into a food processor and blend until smooth.

For the caramelized apple, peel and core the apples, and then quarter them. Melt the butter and sugar over low-medium heat for about 1 minute, until the sugar dissolves and the mixture is bubbly. Add apples and lemon juice and cook over medium heat for approximately 6 to 8 minutes, stirring constantly. Strain, cool and add the apple pieces along with the hazelnut brittle as garnish.

Serves 10

HAZELNUT BRITTLE

2¼ lb/1kg blanched hazelnuts
2¼ cups/500 g sugar
2 tsp (1 dessertspoon) water

Toast the hazelnuts on a baking pan and allow to cool. Place the sugar and water in a pan (making sure to wash down any sugar off the sides) then place on the heat, bringing the sugar to a light caramel stage. Then pour it onto a silicone mat and allow to cool. Once the caramel has cooled, place it into a food processor with the toasted hazelnuts and blend to a fine dust. Place a rectangle cutout flat on a nonstick mat, put the dust into a fine sieve and sprinkle onto the cutout. Then remove the cutout and place the pan in the oven at 200°F/100°C/ Gas Mark ¼ until the sugar has melted clear. Remove from the oven and allow to cool before removing it from the mat.

Serves 8 to 10

Lough Erne Pork Dish

FOR THE PORK FILLET
12 oz/300 g pork fillet
2 oz/40 g Prosciutto crudo (uncooked)

Preheat oven to 165°F/74°C.

Trim the pork fillet, removing any fat. Then cut into 4 pieces. Wrap each piece in the prosciutto and then in plastic wrap tied tight to hold the shape. Refrigerate overnight.

Remove from refrigerator. Put prosciutto-covered pork in a roasting pan and roast in the preheated oven for 45 minutes.

FOR THE PORK BELLY
3 lb 5 oz/1.5 kg pork belly
2 cloves garlic
½ tsp thyme
1 tsp salt

Place the garlic, thyme, and ½ teaspoon of the salt in a food processor and blend until quite fine. Then fold in the remaining salt. Rub onto the pork belly. Wrap tight in plastic wrap and place between two heavy plates or trays to compress. Transfer to the refrigerator for 24 hours. Press occasionally while chilling.

Preheat oven to 180°F/82°C.

Remove the pork from the refrigerator, remove the plastic wrap, and rinse the pork in cold water.

Dry the pork and place, skin side up, in a roasting pan in the preheated oven for 12 hours.

FOR THE BLACK PUDDING PALMIER
½ cup/125 g black pudding
1 clove garlic
½ tsp thyme
4 oz/100 g puff pastry

Preheat oven to 325°F/160°C/Gas Mark 3.

Blend to a paste the black pudding, garlic, and thyme leaves. Place the puff pastry on a parchment paper covered surface with a long side facing you. Spread the black pudding mix across the dough. Roll the

NOTE: Black pudding in Ireland is a blood sausage mixed with oatmeal, a mainstay of a full Irish breakfast and the Ulster fry. And it is no longer served only at breakfast.

dough lengthwise into a long cylinder, as tightly as possible without stretching it, stopping at the middle. Repeat with the other long side to get 2 tight cylinders that meet in the middle. Wrap tightly in plastic wrap; place in the refrigerator to chill for at least 1 hour. Remove from the refrigerator, unwrap the dough, and with a sharp knife, cut the dough crosswise into ⅜-inch-thick slices. Place the palmiers on a nonstick baking pan, flatten with the palm of your hand and bake in the preheated oven for 10 to 15 minutes.

FOR THE APPLE BUTTER
2 lb cooking apples
2–3 tbsp sugar (depending on sweetness of apples)

Peel, core, and coarsely chop the apples. Place into a pot with the sugar and a little water. Cook until dark brown, then blend in a food processor until smooth.

To serve, place the pork loin, the pork belly, and black pudding palmiere on a plate and add a few spoonfuls of the apple butter as a garnish. There are other items in the photo, but the pork, palmier and apple butter are the core of the dish.

Serves 8 to 10

NOTE: When I cook at home I would not include all of the ingredients here. This is the special signature dish at Lough Erne. At home I would prepare the pork loin, palmier, and maybe the pork belly if available. We have given the recipe here for the restaurant style. But please create your own style with the basic recipe. If you eliminate one cut of meat, remember to adjust the quantity of the one you are serving.

Raspberry Cheesecake

8–10 digestive biscuits, crumbled
4 gelatin leaves or 1 envelope of powdered gelatin
Generous 1 cup/250 ml cream
18 oz/500 g raspberry purée
2⅔ cups/600 g cream cheese
3¼ cups/400 g confectioners' sugar

Line individual cheesecake rings with a layer of crumbled biscuits.

Soak the gelatin leaves in iced water, or add the gelatin powder to ¼ cup of cold water. Whip the cream and set aside.

NOTE: For the photograph we added a piped twist of chocolate for fun.

Heat a little of the raspberry purée and dissolve the gelatin into it. Whisk together the cream cheese and confectioners' sugar in a medium-size bowl. Add the remaining raspberry purée and the raspberry purée with the gelatine added. Scrape down the sides of the bowl to ensure the mixture is well blended. Fold in the whipped cream.

Crumble the biscuits and line 4 ramekins with the crumble. Add the raspberry cheesecake mixture on top of the crumble. Chill in the refrigerator for 1 hour or more.

Serve with a scoop of ice cream or sorbet and, if on a summery day, strawberry lemonade.

Serves 4

STRAWBERRY LEMONADE

Capture the flavor and juiciness of strawberries and lemons in this refreshing homemade strawberry lemonade. Make sure you chill the serving pitcher well beforehand and have plenty of strawberry slices, lemon wedges, mint leaves, and crushed ice ready.

9 oz/250 g (about 12 large) strawberries
4 lemons
⅔ cup/150 g superfine sugar
4¼ cups/1 L water, divided

Blend 8 oz/200g of strawberries in a food processor until smooth. Place in a large heatproof pitcher. Thinly peel the zest from the lemons with a vegetable peeler, leaving as much white pith behind as possible. Squeeze the juice from the lemons. Place the zest, lemon juice, and sugar in the large heatproof pitcher with the strawberry mix.

Boil 2½ cups/590 ml water, add to the pitcher, and stir until the sugar has totally dissolved. Cover, and leave to cool completely.

When cool, strain the mixture into a chilled pitcher, and discard the zest. Dilute with 1¾ cups/420 ml chilled water and sweeten with extra sugar to taste. Serve decorated with strawberry slices, lemon slices, or mint leaves in a glass with crushed ice.

Serves 4

TO MAKE A RASPBERRY PURÉE:
Place 4 cups of raspberries in a stainless steel saucepan over medium heat, add up to 4 oz (depending on your taste preference) of superfine sugar and 2 tbsp of lemon juice. Once the raspberries have softened, bring to a boil and cook for a few minutes until the mixture has thickened slightly. Push the mixture through a sieve into a clean bowl, pressing hard to remove the seeds. Refrigerate until ready to serve. Extra purée freezes well.

Crab and Scallops with Seaweed-Avocado Purée and Fresh Lemon Curd

NOTE: For this dish here at Lough Erne we are using Liscanner crab, Ballycastle scallops, and Rathlin Islander seaweed.

NOTE: For this photograph we flattened the crabmeat mixture on plastic wrap and rolled it into a long cylinder, wrapping with the plastic wrap, tying each end tight before putting it into the refrigerator. Then, when ready to serve, we removed the plastic wrap and placed the rolled cylinder of crabmeat salad on a plate surrounded by the scallops, seaweed-avocado purée and other garnishes. We present it this way in the restaurant, but I wouldn't necessarily do this at home. A scoop or spoon of the crabmeat surrounded by the seaweed-avocado purée is fine. We garnished with crumbled dried seaweed here, but chopped roasted or carmelized pecan crumble is a pleasing option.

To carmelize the pecans put 3 tbsp of butter in a frying pan, on a medium heat, add 1 cup of pecans and brown them slowly. Add 3 tbsp of sugar (white or brown) and stir to distribute the sugar evenly over the pecans. Stir and flip the pecans over until they are all slightly browned. Remove from the heat, chop and sprinkle on the prepared plate.

FOR THE CRAB
1 lb/450 g cooked crabmeat
1 tbsp chive
1 tbsp flat leaf parsley
2 tbsp chopped shallots
1 lemon
½ lime, juiced
Salt and pepper
1–2 tbsp mayonnaise

FOR THE SEAWEED-AVOCADO PURÉE
1 cup/100 g dried seaweed
2 tbsp spinach
2 avocados, peeled and pitted
1 lemon, juiced
1 lime, juiced
2 tbsp water
2½ tbsp sugar
1 tsp salt

FOR THE LEMON CURD
4 lemons, zest and juice
⅔ cup/150 g sugar
¾ cup/150 g butter
2 eggs + 1 egg yolk
¼ tsp salt
1 tsp lemon juice

4 scallops
Oil, for frying

Seaweed, to garnish

Put the crabmeat in a bowl. Finely slice the chives and parsley, and finely dice the shallots. Zest the lemon and lime and squeeze the juice out of each, removing any seeds. Mix the herbs, shallot, lemon and lime juice and zest into the crabmeat, add 1 tablespoon of mayonnaise, and season with salt and pepper as necessary. Add more mayonnaise as needed to hold the crabmeat salad together. Place in the refrigerator until ready to serve.

Place the scallops on a tray and set aside.

For the seaweed-avocado purée, place seaweed, spinach, avocados, lemon and lime juices, water, sugar, and salt in a food processor and blend until silky smooth.

For the lemon curd, put the lemon zest and juice, the sugar, and butter into a heatproof bowl. Set the bowl over a pan of gently simmering water, making sure the water is not touching the bottom of the bowl. Stir the mixture every now and again until all of the butter has melted. Lightly whisk the eggs and egg yolk and stir them into the lemon mixture. Whisk until all of the ingredients are well combined, then leave to cook for 10 to 13 minutes, stirring every now and then, until the mixture is creamy and thick enough to coat the back of a spoon. Remove the lemon curd from the heat and set aside to cool, stirring occasionally. Once cooled, spoon the lemon curd into sterilized jars and seal with the jar tops. Keep in the refrigerator until ready to use.

To prepare the scallops, heat a heavy-based skillet with a little oil. Place the scallops in the pan in a single layer, spaced about an inch apart. The first scallop placed in the pan should sizzle on contact. If it doesn't, wait a few seconds to let the pan fully heat before adding the rest. Cook the scallops without turning them for 2 to 3 minutes. Then turn them over and cook on the second side for another 2 to 3 minutes without moving. Both sides of the scallop should be seared golden brown and the sides should look opaque all the way through. The scallops should feel firm to the touch, but still slightly soft, like well-set Jello. Don't overcook the scallops or they become tough and chewy.

Place some crabmeat in the center of the plate. Add the scallop, and garnish with samphire, fresh herbs, seaweed purée, and lemon curd.

Serves 4

Fillet of Beef Bourguignon with Mushroom Duxcelles, Pearl Onions, and Roast Beef Sauce

NOTE: This is Kettyle Irish beef we are using.

FOR THE BEEF
2–2¼ lb beef fillet, cut to 6–7 oz fillets
Salt and pepper
1–2 tbsp oil, for sautéing fillets and mushrooms
4 slices Irish smoked bacon
8 pearl onions
½ cup/100 ml beef jus

FOR THE MUSHROOM DUXCELLES
¾ cup/200 g chanterelle mushrooms
1 cup/250 g button mushrooms
5 shallots, sliced fine
3 cloves garlic
1 sprig thyme
1¼ cups/300 ml vegetable stock

FOR THE MASHED POTATOES
1 lb washed and peeled potatoes
4 tbsp butter
3½ fl oz/100 ml cream
2 cloves garlic
1 sprig rosemary
1 sprig thyme
Season to taste

With a sharp knife, cut each fillet crosswise into ¾ in/2 cm-thick slices. Salt and pepper the fillets on both sides. In a large, heavy-bottomed pan on medium-high heat, sauté the slices of beef in batches in 1 tablespoon of oil, adding more as necessary until browned on the outside and very rare inside, about 2 to 3 minutes on each side. Remove the fillets from the pan and set aside on a platter. Very lightly sauté the sliced bacon and pearl onions and remove quickly. Do not let the bacon get crispy. Drain on paper towels.

For the bourguignon garnish, heat the beef jus in the sauté pan just used. Add the pearl onions. Roll the bacon slices and add to the pan. Keep warm until ready to serve.

For the mushroom duxcelles, wash the mushrooms (chanterelle and button), add oil to a sauce pan, and place the sliced shallots, garlic,

FOLLOWING SPREAD: The stunning 600-acre Lough Erne Resort on the shore of Lough Erne. Lough Erne Resort hosted the 39th G8 summit in June 2013.

thyme, and mushrooms to sweat off (cook without browning). Then add in the vegetable stock and further cook the mushrooms. Reserve a few mushrooms to use for garnish. Strain the mushrooms from the stock and place into a blender; mix to a fine chop.

For the mashed potatoes, gently steam the potatoes for about 45 minutes. When soft, push through a ricer, or mash. Heat up the butter, cream, garlic, rosemary, and thyme in a pan until the butter is melted. Push through a sieve on to the mashed potatoes and stir in with a wooden spoon. Season to taste.

To serve, place the mashed potato in the center of the plate with the mushroom duxcelles and bourguignon garnish around it and the fillet of beef on top.

Serves 4

MacNean House and
Restaurant
Blacklion
Co. Cavan
Chef: Neven Maguire

ABOVE: MacNean House and Restaurant in Blacklion, Co. Cavan. In addition to his restaurant and cookery school, Neven has launched his exclusive "Chef's Table with Neven" dining experience where Neven and his team cook in front of diners and present the restaurant's acclaimed Tasting Menu.

Neven Maguire is the award-winning Head Chef/Owner of MacNean House and Restaurant in Blacklion, Co. Cavan. The restaurant, formerly run by his parents, is where he learned to cook. Neven has worked at some top restaurants including Arzac in San Sebastian, Spain (3 Michelin stars). He took over MacNean House and restaurant in 2001, and it is now one of Ireland's top restaurants and a luxury guest house. He is credited with raising international awareness of Ireland's high quality producers.

MENUS

LUNCH

**Cashew Nut Chicken and Asparagus Salad
with Mango Salsa**

Peach Tarte Tatin with Citrus Mascarpone

DINNER ONE

**Crispy Goat Cheese with Apple and
Hazelnut Salad**

**Chicken and Chickpea Tagine with
Honey and Ginger**

Cappuccino Cream Chocolate Cake

DINNER TWO

Steak and Caramelized Onion Open Sandwich

**Spiced Poached Pears with Crème Fraîche
and Toasted Almonds**

Neven is the author of many award-winning cookbooks, and has filmed several television food series which are shown in the UK and on PBS in the US.

ABOVE: Chef Neven Maguire was presented with Ireland's Producer Champion Award. His television series— *Home Chef*—is popular in the UK and on PBS here in the US.

LEFT: Fulfilling a long-held dream, Neven officially opened his Neven Maguire Cookery School next to his restaurant in late 2013. The state-of-the-art cookery school features a range of exciting cookery classes for all skill levels, the popular Parent and Child courses, and tours of Neven's extensive vegetable and herb collection.

Cashew Nut Chicken and Asparagus Salad with Mango Salsa

This delicious salad is packed full of goodness. It can be served simple and rustic, or for a more formal occasion you can arrange the crispy cashew nut chicken in the middle of a plate and garnish with a small mound of dressed baby salad leaves.

FOR THE CHICKEN AND ASPARAGUS SALAD
1 cup/100 g panko—(dried toasted breadcrumbs)
½ cup/75 g toasted cashew nuts
2 tbsp toasted coconut flakes
½ cup/50 g plain flour
1 egg
¼ cup/50 ml milk
2 chicken fillets, each weighing 7 oz/200 g, sliced lengthways
About 1 tsp olive oil spray
1 bunch of asparagus
2 baby romaine lettuces
1 small head radicchio lettuce
Alfalfa sprouts, to garnish

FOR THE MANGO SALSA
1 firm, ripe mango, peeled and diced
1 small red onion, finely diced
Juice of ½ lime
1 tbsp rapeseed oil
1 tbsp chopped fresh cilantro
Sea salt and freshly ground black pepper

Preheat the oven to 350°F/180°C/Gas Mark 4. Line a baking sheet with parchment paper.

Place the panko, cashew nuts, and coconut flakes in a food processor with a pinch of salt. Blend for 2 to 3 minutes, then tip into a shallow dish.

Place the flour in a dish and season with salt and pepper. Whisk the egg and milk together in a separate dish. Dust each slice of chicken in the seasoned flour, then dip into the egg wash and coat in the cashew nut crumbs.

Place the coated chicken strips on the lined baking sheet and spray lightly with the olive oil. Place in the oven for 15 to 20 minutes, until cooked through and golden.

Meanwhile, to make the mango salsa, mix the mango with the red onion, lime juice, rapeseed oil, and cilantro then season to taste and set aside at room temperature.

Break the woody stems off the asparagus and cut each one on the diagonal into two or three pieces, depending on their size. Blanch in a pan of boiling salted water for 2 to 3 minutes, until just tender, but still with a little bite. Drain and refresh under cold running water.

Trim down the romaine and radicchio, then break into separate leaves and put in a large bowl with the blanched asparagus. Arrange in shallow bowls and place the cashew nut chicken strips on top. Spoon around the mango salsa and add the alfalfa sprouts to garnish.

Serves 4

Peach Tarte Tatin with Citrus Mascarpone

3 ripe peaches
4 tbsp butter
¼ cup/50 g superfine sugar
2 tbsp cream
1 tbsp brandy
1 package puff pastry, thawed if frozen

CITRUS MASCARPONE
½ tsp finely grated orange rind
½ tsp finely grated lemon rind
2 tbsp fresh orange juice
½ cup/100 g mascarpone cheese
1–2 tbsp sifted confectioners' sugar

This is a very impressive dessert to get done in such a short time but is definitely achievable by using the ready-to-roll puff pastry. Look out for the all butter version, which more supermarkets are now stocking.

Preheat the oven to 425°F/220°C/Gas Mark 7 and preheat the grill.

Place the peaches in a pan of boiling water for 1 minute, remove, then plunge into cold water and peel away the skins. Cut into halves and remove the pits, then cut into quarters.

Meanwhile, melt the butter with the sugar in a small pan. Bring to a boil and simmer for 5 to 6 minutes, beating continuously until thickened and lightly golden. Remove from the heat, leave to cool for 1 minute, then stir in the cream, beating until smooth. Spoon into a shallow 8 in/20 cm tart pan. Arrange the peach quarters on top, cut side up, and drizzle over the brandy.

Unroll the puff pastry on a clean work surface and cut out a 10 in/ 25 cm round. Place over the peaches, pushing the edges down the side of the pan; trim off any excess pastry. Place on a baking sheet and bake for 15 to 20 minutes until golden brown.

Meanwhile, to make the citrus mascarpone, beat the orange and lemon rind into the mascarpone and then stir in the orange juice. Add enough of the confectioners' sugar to sweeten.

Loosen the puff pastry from the pan with a knife. Cool, then turn on to a heatproof dish and place under the broiler just long enough to gratinate the top until caramelized. Serve cut into slices on warmed plates with quenelles or spoonfuls of the citrus mascarpone.

Serves 4

Crispy Goat Cheese with Apple and Hazelnut Salad

FOR THE GOAT CHEESE

2 tbsp fresh white
    breadcrumbs
1 tbsp finely chopped fresh
    flat-leaf parsley
1 tbsp sesame seeds
2 tsp very finely chopped,
    skinned, and toasted
    hazelnuts
1 egg
2 tbsp plain flour
Sea salt and freshly ground
    black pepper
5 oz/150 g Irish (if possible)
    goat cheese, cut into
    4 slices
Sunflower oil, for deep-frying

FOR THE SALAD

2 crisp apples
Juice of 1 lemon
1 bunch arugula leaves
2 tbsp extra-virgin olive oil
4 tbsp skinned, toasted
    hazelnuts, roughly
    chopped

Preheat the oven to
350°F/180°C/Gas Mark 4.

To prepare the crispy goat cheese, mix the breadcrumbs with the parsley, sesame seeds, and chopped hazelnuts in a shallow dish and season to taste.

In a separate dish, beat the egg and season lightly. Season the flour and place in another shallow dish.

Lightly coat the goat cheese in the seasoned flour, then dip each slice into the beaten egg, gently shaking off any excess. Place in the breadcrumb mixture so that they are completely coated. Set on a baking sheet lined with parchment paper and place in the refrigerator for at least 10 minutes to firm up.

Heat the oil in a deep-sided pan or deep-fat fryer to 350°F/180°C and cook the breaded goat cheese for 1 to 2 minutes, until golden brown.

Carefully remove from the oil and transfer to a plate lined with paper towels to drain off any excess oil. Arrange back on the lined baking sheet and place in the oven for 3 to 4 minutes, until heated through but still holding their shape.

Meanwhile, make the apple and hazelnut salad. Using a mandolin or a very sharp knife, cut the apples into wafer-thin slices and toss in the lemon juice to prevent discoloration. Cover each plate with a layer of slightly overlapping apple slices and add a small mound of the arugula, then drizzle with olive oil. Put the crispy goat cheese into the center of each plate and scatter over the hazelnuts to serve.

Serves 4

Chicken and Chickpea Tagine with Honey and Ginger

The combination of spicy chicken, tomatoes, and chickpeas here is really successful, and the best thing about it is that it all gets cooked in the one pot so there's very little washing up.

NOTE: I've suggested serving it with steamed couscous, but bulghar wheat or—if you want to be really trendy—quinoa would be equally delicious. And don't dress the dish with just lemon. In Morocco they use everything from sultanas to bananas and/or toasted nuts, as the essence of their cooking is the exquisite combination of fruit and nuts.

8 large skinless boneless chicken thighs or 4 skinless boneless breasts
½ tsp ground paprika
½ tsp ground turmeric
½ tsp ground cinnamon
1 tsp ground ginger
1 tsp cayenne pepper
1 tbsp clear honey
3 tbsp olive oil
1 small red onion, finely sliced
2 garlic cloves, finely chopped
2 ripe tomatoes, peeled, seeded, and chopped
2¼ cups chickpeas (400 g), drained and rinsed
15 fl oz/450 ml chicken stock
Juice of ½ lemon
2 tbsp chopped fresh cilantro
1 tbsp chopped fresh mint
Sea salt and freshly ground black pepper
Steamed green herby couscous, to serve (optional)

Trim down the chicken and cut into bite-size pieces. Place in a bowl with the spices, honey, and one tablespoon of the oil. Season generously, then stir well to combine and set aside for at least 5 minutes to allow the flavors to develop.

Heat the remaining 2 tablespoons of oil in a sauté pan with a lid, then sauté the onion and garlic for 4 to 5 minutes until softened and just beginning to brown. Add the marinated chicken and sauté for a minute or two until just sealed and lightly browned.

Add half of the tomatoes to the pan with the stock and chickpeas, then bring to the boil. Reduce the heat, cover and simmer for 10 to 12 minutes or until the chicken is completely tender and the sauce has slightly thickened, stirring occasionally. Season to taste.

Stir the remaining tomatoes into the pan and season to taste, then add the lemon juice, cilantro, and mint. Stir to combine and arrange on warmed plates with the herby green couscous, if liked.

Serves 4

Cappuccino Cream Chocolate Cake

1⅔ cups/200 g confectioners' sugar, sifted
1¾ lb/750 g mascarpone cheese, well chilled
1 vanilla bean, split in half and seeds scraped out
15 fl oz/450 ml cream, well chilled
7 fl oz/200 ml freshly brewed strong espresso coffee (left to cool)
3½ fl oz/100 ml Coole Swan® liqueur
2 chocolate loaf cakes, 380 g each (store-bought or homemade)
Cocoa powder, to dust
10–12 chocolate-covered coffee beans
2 tsp cocoa powder (good quality)

Using an electric whisk, mix the confectioners' sugar, mascarpone cheese, and vanilla seeds until well combined. Whip 13 fl oz (375ml) of the cream until soft peaks form and then fold into the mascarpone mixture.

Pour the coffee into a shallow dish and stir in the Coole Swan. Slice the chocolate loaves. Line the base and sides of a 9 in (23 cm) spring-form cake tin with parchment paper and wrap the outside in plastic wrap to avoid any leaks.

Dip 8 of the chocolate cake slices in the Coole Swan mixture to cover the bottom of the tin. It is important to only dip them in as you go along so they are not soaking for long and difficult to handle.

Cover the layer of soaked chocolate cake with a third of the mascarpone cream and then arrange another even layer of the soaked cake slices on top. Continue layering in this way finishing with a mascarpone layer and place in the refrigerator to chill for 10 to 15 minutes.

When ready to serve, whip the rest of the cream in a clean bowl and transfer to a piping bag fitted with a star-shape nozzle. Carefully remove from the cake tin and transfer to a cake stand. Give the cake a good even dusting of the cocoa powder and then pipe 10 to 12 peaks of cream around the edge of the cake and top each one with a chocolate-covered coffee bean. Place in the middle of the table so that everyone can help themselves.

Serves 10 to 12

This might look like a very impressive cake that took ages to make but it's really only an assembly job. Mascarpone is a rich, creamy cheese originating from Lodi in the Lombardy region of Italy. It has a sweetened taste and is famously used in a classic Tiramisu, which is the basis of this dessert. However I've used shop-bought chocolate loaf cakes instead of the traditional sponge fingers.

NOTE: Coole Swan® liqueur is made with Irish whiskey, chocolate and cream. If unavailable you could add a liqueur of your choice.

Steak and Caramelized Onion Open Sandwich

There are times when you want something tasty and delicious but just don't feel like cooking a full meal. This is one of those dishes you'll find yourself cooking again and again. If you want to make it even more substantial, try serving it with french fries and watch how quickly the plates are cleared!

3 tbsp olive oil
2 large red onions, sliced and separated into rings
1 tbsp light muscovado sugar, or light brown sugar
1 tbsp balsamic vinegar
2 thin-cut rump or sirloin steaks, each 6 oz/175 g
1 small ciabatta loaf

4 tbsp mayonnaise
1 tsp Dijon mustard
1 tsp whole-grain mustard
2 ripe tomatoes, sliced
1 bunch arugula
Sea salt and freshly ground black pepper

Heat 2 tablespoons of the oil in a large frying pan and preheat the grill. Fry onions for 10 minutes until softened and golden, stirring occasionally. Sprinkle over the sugar and balsamic vinegar and then cook for another 2 minutes until the sugar has dissolved and is slightly syrupy, stirring continuously. Tip into a bowl and keep warm.

Return the pan to the heat and add the remaining tablespoon of oil. Season the steaks, add them to the pan, and cook over a high heat for 3 to 4 minutes on each side for well done; or according to taste.

Split the ciabatta in half and then arrange on the broiler pan, cut side up. Place under the broiler until lightly toasted. Mix the mayonnaise in a small bowl with the two mustards.

Place a piece of the toasted ciabatta on each warmed serving plate. Add a smear of the mustard mayonnaise and then arrange a layer of the tomato slices. Season to taste and add the arugula. Place the steak on top and add the reserved caramelized onions. Drizzle over the rest of the mustard mayonnaise to serve.

Serves 4

Spiced Poached Pears with Crème Fraîche and Toasted Almonds

This delightful dessert will revive even the most jaded palate. The pears improve with keeping, making this an excellent dessert for entertaining. Choose fruit that is perfectly ripe but still quite firm so the flesh doesn't go mushy while you are preparing them.

1¼ cups/300 ml clear apple juice
Juice and finely grated rind of 2 limes
2 whole star anise
1 cinnamon stick, broken in half
½ vanilla bean, split in half
2 tbsp honey
4 firm, ripe pears
2 tbsp toasted flaked almonds
½ cup/100 g crème fraîche

Place the apple juice in a deep-sided pan with a lid (the pan needs to be just large enough to hold the pears in an upright position). Add the lime juice and rind, star anise, cinnamon stick, vanilla pod, and honey. Bring to a boil, then reduce the heat and simmer gently for a few minutes to allow the flavors to infuse.

Meanwhile, peel the pears, leaving the stalks attached.

Add them to the pan, standing them in an upright position. Cover with the lid and simmer gently for 20 to 25 minutes, until the pears are tender, basting them from time to time with the liquid. Remove from the heat and leave to cool in the syrup. The cooking time will depend on the ripeness of the pears.

Using a slotted spoon, transfer the pears to a dish and set aside. Reduce the cooking juices by half to a more syrupy consistency. This will take 8 to 12 minutes. Strain into a pitcher and leave to cool.

To serve, carefully cut each pear in half so that you don't spoil their beautiful shape. Place the pear halves on a serving platter and drizzle over the spiced syrup. Scatter over the toasted flaked almonds and serve with a separate bowl of crème fraîche.

Serves 4

St. George's Market in Belfast

St. George's Market in Belfast, built between 1890 and 1896, is one of the best markets in the UK and Ireland and a popular visitor's site. It has received numerous local and national awards for its fresh, local produce and a great atmosphere. Approximately 248 market stalls sell a variety of products on Friday, Saturday, and Sunday from fruit and vegetables, fish, meat, cheese, clothing, local crafts, books and artwork. Local bands entertain, and local craftspeople offer their goods for sale.

Recipes by Chef

The chefs own the copyrights to their own recipes as listed below.

DERRY CLARKE © 2017
L'Ecrivain

LUNCH
Crispy Duck Breast with Glazed Butternut Squash and Star Anise Jus
Lemon Curd with Meringue and Raspberries

STARTER
Vodka-Cured Irish Salmon with Avocado Cream, Pickled Vegetables, and Horseradish Mayonnaise
Cod, Octopus, Purple Broccoli, Broccoli Purée, and Horseradish Mayonnaise

MAIN COURSE
Beef Fillet and Brisket with Morels and Mushroom Purée
Venison with Puréed Celeriac and Spinach

DESSERT
Pear Mille Feuille
Chocolate Mousse with Walnut Ganache

CATHERINE FULVIO © 2017
Ballyknocken Cookery School

LUNCH
Orange, Spinach, and Salmon Salad

TEA
Ballyknocken Tea Scones
Guinness® Chocolate Cupcakes

STARTER
Carrot, Potato, and Cumin Soup
Seared Lamb and Beetroot Salad

MAIN COURSE
Beef and Wicklow Wolf Stout Casserole with Dumplings
Salmon and Leek Pie

DESSERT
Apple and Mango Crumble
Irish Mint Truffle Torte with Irish Mist Cream

KEVIN DUNDON © 2017
Dunbrody House

LUNCH
Potato, Prawn, and Lime Soup
Paupiette of Sole and Crabmeat

TEA
Victoria Sponge with Strawberries

STARTER
Lobster Buttered Soup
Scallops and Caviar with Nasturtium Coulis

MAIN COURSE
Chicken Ballotines with Potato Farls
Slow-Cooked Shoulder of Pork with Stuffing, Sautéed Potatoes, and Apple Compote

DESSERT
Wexford Berries with Mini Meringues
Buttermilk and Heather-Infused Panna Cotta

DARINA ALLEN © 2017
Ballymaloe Cookery School

LUNCH
Warm Salad of Gubbeen Bacon with Poached Egg and Coolea Cheese
Smoked Salmon with Cucumber Pickle

TEA
Florence Bowe's Crumpets

STARTER
Ballycotton Shrimp with Homemade Wild Garlic Mayonnaise
Ballymaloe Brown Yeast Bread
Carpaccio of Scallops with Chili, Lemon, and Wood Sorrel

MAIN COURSE
Roast Lamb with Mint Sauce and Glazed Carrots
Poached Salmon with Irish Butter Sauce

DESSERT
Carrageen Moss Pudding
Spring Rhubarb Tart with Crystallized Ginger Cream

MARTIN BEALIN © 2017
Global Village

LUNCH
Dingle Bay Scallops, Poached Eggs, Potato Cakes, and Burnt Butter Hollandaise, with Pickled Cucumber
Goat Cheese Mousse, Beet Chutney, Caramelized Hazelnuts, and Apple Crisps

STARTER
Trio of Local Brown Crab: Crab Parfait, Crabmeat and Apple Salad, and Bisque Shot
Smoked Duck Breast with Duck Liver Pâté and Sultana and Apple Chutney

MAIN COURSE
West Kerry Lamb: Braised Lamb with Pearl Barley Risotto
Seared Dingle Bay Scallops, Pea Purée, Pork Breast, and Apple Crisps

DESSERT

Buttermilk Posset with Almond Biscuits

Rhubarb Crumble with Salted Caramel
Ice Cream

ULTAN COOKE © 2017
Ballynahinch Castle

LUNCH

Whipped Goat Cheese with Beet Slaw
and Apple Syrup

STARTER

Sea Scallops with Puréed and Pickled
Cauliflower

Wood Pigeon, Gooseberry, and Spinach

MAIN COURSE

Lamb, Samphire, and Burnt Onion
Purée

Sweaty Betty with Barley and Seaweed

DESSERT

Rose Water Crème Brûlée

Sheep Yogurt Mousse with Marinated
Strawberries and Mint

TIM O'SULLIVAN © 2017
Renvyle House

LUNCH

Scallops on a Pea Purée with Vegetable
Butter Sauce and Crispy Pancetta

Homemade Pork and Apple Sausage
with Shallot and Sage Mashed
Potatoes and Port Jus

TEA

Chocolate Steamed Pudding

STARTER

Mussel Pie with Chive Mashed Potatoes

West Coast Seafood Chowder

MAIN COURSE

Atlantic Way Duet: Rack of Lamb and
Atlantic Lobster with Spinach
and Tomato Fondue

Crispy Breast of Duckling with
Root Vegetables

DESSERT

Renvyle House Berry Trifle

Rhubarb and Ginger Crème Brûlée

IAN ORR © 2017
Browns

LUNCH

Goat Cheese, Endive, and Walnut
Salad

Pork Fillet with Roasted Butternut
Squash, Mushrooms, Lemon,
and Parsley

STARTER

Seared Scallops with Black Pudding
Crumb and Homemade Potato
Bread

Gin-Cured Salmon and Pickled
Cucumber with Dill

MAIN COURSE

Beef Fillet with Buttered Spinach,
Dulse Seaweed Hollandaise

Lamb with Spinach, Goat Curd Cheese,
and Toasted Pine Nuts

DESSERT

Chocolate Fondant

Vanilla Panna Cotta with Honeycomb

NOEL McMEEL © 2017
Lough Erne Resort

LUNCH

Traditional Fish and Chips

Smoked Irish Salmon, Cream Cheese,
and Traditional Boxty

STARTER

Roast Artichoke Soup with
Caramelized Armagh Apple and
Hazelnut Brittle

Crab and Scallops with Seaweed-
Avocado Purée and Fresh
Lemon Curd

MAIN COURSE

Lough Erne Pork Dish

Fillet of Beef Bourguignon with
Mushroom Duxcelles, Pearl Onions,
and Roast Beef Sauce

DESSERT

Raspberry Cheesecake and Strawberry
Lemonade

NEVEN MAGUIRE © 2017
MacNean House

LUNCH

Cashew Nut Chicken and Asparagus
Salad with Mango Salsa

Peach Tarte Tatin with Citrus
Mascarpone

STARTER

Crispy Goat Cheese with Apple and
Hazelnut Salad

MAIN COURSE

Chicken and Chickpea Tagine with
Honey and Ginger

Steak and Caramelized Onion Open
Sandwich

DESSERT

Cappuccino Cream Chocolate Cake

Spiced Poached Pears with Crème
Fraîche and Toasted Almonds

Index

Photo Credits

Martin Bealin: 108 top, 112

Chris Hill/Scenic Ireland: Pages 2 bottom left and right, 6 bottom, 7 top and bottom, 9 top and bottom, 10-Derry Clarke, 11-Ian Orr, Noel McMeel, 12–13, 15 top and bottom, 16, 17 top and bottom, 21, 23, 24, 25, 26, 27, 29, 31, 32, 33, 39, 40, 43, 45, 47, 48, 51, 53, 54, 76–77, 79, 80–81, 106, 107, 118, 128, 129, 130 top and bottom, 132–133, 144, 172–173, 174, 175 bottom, 176 top and bottom, 177 top and bottom, 179 top, 180, 181, 183, 184, 185, 186, 187, 189, 191, 192, 195, 197 top and bottom, 199, 200, 202, 203, 205, 206, 209, 211, 212–213, 230, 240

Carsten Krieger: Pages 6 top, 8, 10-Darina Allen, Ultan Cooke, Kevin Dundon, 11-Tim O'Sullivan, 14, 56, 57 top, 58, 59, 61, 63, 64, 67, 69, 70, 71, 73, 78, 82 top, 83 top, 84, 85, 87, 88, 91, 92, 96, 97, 98, 99, 103, 104, 105, 111, 113, 114, 117, 119, 120, 123, 124, 125, 133 top, 134, 136, 137, 138–139, 141, 145, 147, 149, 151, 152–153, 154, 155 top, 156, 157, 158, 159, 160, 163, 164, 167, 169, 171, 175 top, 188, 193, 205

Paul Lindsay/Scenic Ireland: Pages 106, 107

Joanne Murphy: Pages 11-Neven Maguire, 214, 215 top and bottom, 217, 219, 220, 223, 224, 227, 228

Don MacMonagle: Pages 10-Martin Bealin, 108, 109 top and bottom

Courtesy Ballyknocken Cookery School: Catherine Fulvio: Pages 11 top, 16, 17
Courtesy Ballymaloe Cookery School: Pages 82 bottom, 83 bottom, 101
Courtesy Ballynahinch Castle: Pages 134, 135
Courtesy Browns Restaurant: Pages 178, 179 bottom
Courtesy Dunbrody House: Pages 57 bottom, 62, 72
Courtesy Gubbeen Farm, Fingal Ferguson: Pages 86-87
Courtesy Lough Erne Resort: Page 196
Courtesy Murphy's Ice Cream: Pages 126, 127
Courtesy Renvyle House: Page 155 bottom
Courtesy Tourism Ireland: irelandscontentpool: Pages 74, 75, 93, 148, 150, 166, 221, 231

Acknowledgments

Thank you to each of the chefs for offering their recipes with permission to use them in this book.

Thank you to the following for assistance:
Diana Cantor from L'Ecrivain; Julien Clémot, Niamh Donegan from Dunbrody House; Sharon Hogan at Ballymaloe Cookery School; Jane Walsh and Shauna McTigue from Ballynahinch; Andrea Doherty from MacNean House. Thank you to Tourism Ireland, especially Ruth Moran, New York; to Peter Harbison in Dublin, to photographers Carsten Krieger in Loop Head and Chris Hill in Belfast. Martin Bealin would like to thank Michael Boyle, Louise Brosnan, Derren McNulty, Jordan Carey, and Paudi Ryan from Global Village for "making the whole thing possible." A special thank you to Mary Ann Sabia, publisher at Charlesbridge Publishing, with her gracious patience for a complex project, and to Don Weise, acquisitions editor. Thanks to Debby Zindell. And thank you and case of champagne to Lori S. Malkin for making this possible.